THERE IS ALWAYS HOPE

THERE IS ALWAYS HOPE

Ordinary people cast into extraordinary circumstances

Colin Campbell

Troubador Publishing Ltd
Unit E2 Airfield Business Park
Harrison Road, Market Harborough
Leicestershire LE16 7UL
Tel: 0116 279 2299
Email: books@troubador.co.uk
Web: www.troubador.co.uk

ISBN 978 1 8051 4328 4

British Library Cataloguing in Publication Data.
A catalogue record for this book is available from the British Library.

Printed and bound in Great Britain by 4edge Limited
Typeset in 11pt Minion Pro by Troubador Publishing Ltd, Leicester, UK

Dedicated to Deidre

Acknowledgements

Firstly, humble thanks to Deidre for agreeing to let me to write this story. She had been reluctant as she is a very private person, but she was persuaded in the hope that it might be of help to others going through a similar experience.

Heartfelt thanks to the oncologists, pharmacists, radiologists, nurses and support staff of the North West Cancer Centre whose devotion and professionalism leave me speechless. Their endless help and support have been so important to us, particularly in the early days when we needed that assistance most. We are grateful also to the MacMillan Cancer Support and Making 2nds Count charities and all their volunteers who were there for us when we needed them. The charities work tirelessly to support cancer sufferers and their families.

Thanks to our friends Kathy, Rachel, Caroline, Pulna, Chris and Kathleen who took the time and trouble to read drafts of the book at its various stages and provide valuable input and advice.

I am so grateful to our family members, particularly Deidre's mother, universally known as Sheila, Conan, Aidan, and Suzanne for their support throughout the process, and to Connie for being quite simply an inspiration.

Immense thanks also to Derek, my brother, and his family for their support particularly as we came to terms with our mother's passing at the height of lockdown. Also to my close friends Stephen and Paul for listening and keeping me focused throughout this time, even if that focus was lost occasionally through a few glasses of wine! Thanks also to a long list of friends, you know who you are, whose love and support carried us during those early dark days.

Thanks also to my publisher, particularly Beth and Raisa, who have guided me through the process with empathy and patience. It has certainly been an experience for me and I could not have done it without you.

Finally, I would like to mention my mum and dad who allowed me the freedom to become the person I am and I remain truly grateful for their endless love and support throughout all the stages of my life.

Prologue

Well maybe just one, I thought with no little glee as I approached the hotel near where we lived. I had left Deidre to the beautician to have her nails done, or something like that, as we prepared for our first skiing holiday together, only four days away. To be accurate, it was *my* first, as she and the boys had been away a few times and were, therefore, quite experienced. I had never skied before, and I was nervous – of making a fool of myself, that is. I was not that young any more, and my chest had recently been giving me a little more bother than usual. But, hey, it would all be okay. Of course it would. It was a holiday, for heaven's sake, and it started now, and if I made headway I might even have time for two. Life was good. Life could be excellent.

I drove into the car park and pulled up near the entrance, which was on quite a steep slope. For no apparent reason, I thought of how older people, no doubt with respiratory problems, might have difficulty getting from their cars to the entrance, and then reasoned that those in most need would probably not be driving anyway and would be left at the front door by a good Samaritan.

"No such luxury for me," I whispered to myself as I smiled the smile of someone about to go on holiday. But then, I was still young, and in a week's time I would have a new set of photos of myself in skiing gear to add to my James Bond fantasy collection – my secret James Bond fantasy collection, that is.

"The holiday starts now!" I said out loud in the knowledge that no one would hear me. I took the keys out of the ignition, handbrake already on, and lifted my mobile phone from the passenger seat. As I did, I noticed the tab telling me I had three new messages. I had put the phone on silent, and rather than wait until I was seated with a glass in front of me, I decided to open them before I walked to the door. *Probably about the house*, I thought, as I hoped to be nearing the sale of my property and freedom from the debt that had grown enough to plague me since my divorce seven years earlier.

"Hi, it's John. Give me a call when you can on this number." It was, indeed, my estate agent. He was a good fellow, and I wished I had known about him when I'd first decided to sell instead of wasting time with the other crew. John shared my view that my house was a palace in which someone else would soon have the honour of living. I wasn't sure if it was good news as I pressed play for message number two – John was blessed with a deadpan delivery style, regardless of his message.

"Colin, give me a call on this number when you can?" John again. Maybe something was moving after all, and I pressed the button to listen to number three, fully expecting it to be John yet again, and was therefore only half listening, as I did not intend to be calling him back this evening. More exciting things were about to happen, and I could almost taste the Sauvignon Blanc on my tongue.

"Mr Campbell, it's Alan from the Causeway Hospital, Coleraine. Could you call me urgently please?" Just then, and not because of the slope, I fell back into the car, banging my head on the edge of the passenger seat. As if the call hadn't been shock enough. Naturally, with these messages, there was no call-back number, and as I was not on Wi-Fi, my not-so-smart phone was responding slower than normal and much, much slower than I pleaded with it to. After googling – I believe it has been awarded verb status – every Causeway Hospital website I could find, I finally came across a number that looked like the one I needed and dialled frantically. I am not at my best when in panic mode. Ask my solicitor. In fact, better, ask my ex-wife's solicitor. After three rings, the recorded message informed me that they were closed for the evening and would open again at eight in the morning, thanking me ever so politely for calling. My heart was racing, thumping through my shirt, and I felt physically ill, fear taking over me as my breathing increased in pace, wheezing, and my skin felt like it was frying. As I was in no condition to drive, I went into the hotel bar and ordered a cup of tea.

There was almost a look of confusion mixed with surprise and disappointment on the woman's face as she took my order. I obviously have the look of a drinker. Or maybe she simply remembered me.

"Certainly, sir," she responded, as if I had asked her to wax my chest hair. I did not wait for the tea to arrive but went immediately to the men's toilets, and, luckily, no one else was there. I stood and looked at the mirror, probably for about five minutes. I am not sure what I was looking for. I am not sure what I was even looking at, but I tried to calm myself as much as I possibly could by inventing a series of reasons as to why they had called, leaving out, of course, the most obvious one. There was, however, last week's CT scan, and it refused to be omitted from my list of reasons for the call. Due largely to the excitement and anticipation of the forthcoming holiday, I had been able to put it to the back of my mind, and I had been very relaxed about it, dismissing it as a simple check-up they have to do to keep everything in order and fulfil their administrative obligations. But the CT scan, it appeared, had not forgotten about me. I paid my bill for the tea, leaving without touching a drop, and when asked if everything was okay, I deliberately mumbled something short and incoherent to hasten my escape.

When I collected Deidre, I said nothing on the short journey home and even considered keeping quiet until I had spoken with the hospital in the morning. But it only took one "What's wrong?" from her for me to crumble and spill the beans. Suddenly, rather than being excited in anticipation of a holiday, I felt exhausted and fearful, and the look on Deidre's face did not help. I had been hoping for a more reassuring response, allowing me to conclude that everything would be okay. Not this. God love her, she was as shocked as I was, and to be fair, I gave her no opportunity to mask her reaction. Death never actually seems to happen to anyone close to us unless it is their time, as we say. But it was not my time, so her reaction was both appealing and frightening. It was not my time to die, but it didn't mean I wouldn't.

During dinner I fiddled about with my food and, having surrendered to a lack of appetite, spent the evening searching the Internet – the one thing they tell you not to do – for hope or assurance of any kind. But everywhere I looked it was not good. Did I have lung cancer, or chronic obstructive pulmonary disease, COPD to you and me, which the doctor had mentioned during the most recent diagnosis of my breathing problems? COPD means that the lungs are damaged in a way that causes shortness of breath, a persistent chesty cough with phlegm that does not go away, frequent chest infections and persistent wheezing, with the symptoms usually becoming worse over time, making daily activities increasingly difficult.

Despite this, compared to cancer, COPD seemed quite desirable. I found stories on the Internet of COPD sufferers completing marathons and other similar achievements, and this was encouraging, as I use the treadmill almost every day. But lung cancer? That was different.

Little time, no cure, no chance. I became consumed by the idea that my regular drinking must have caused this, not to mention my old smoking habit, both of which must have contributed to my asthma condition, which had been exacerbated by cat allergies. How on earth could there not be anything wrong with me? I could hardly breathe half the time, and my only success was in being able to hide the severity of the condition from others and, probably, myself. *Why me*? I asked. It was obvious, wasn't it?

Several months earlier, in the steam room of the local gym of all places, I met a minister who had taken the funeral service of the young wife of a work colleague whose premature death left him to bring up their two little boys on his own. In this strangest of all environments, and completely out of character, I mentioned this to the minister, who thankfully remembered the people in question and in the brief follow-up conversation recalled the fact that, especially when victims are young, family and friends will often say "Why me?" when an equally valid question is "Why not me?" I always remembered that, cold as it seemed at the time. And now, "Why not me?" I'd had pneumonia three times, had been a casual smoker and was a regular user of inhalers for my asthma condition. It just had to be me.

During the night, I didn't sleep at all and can remember both hands of the clock signalling every hour on the hour while I played over various scenarios, most of which did not end well. As something of an expert in dreaming up unhappy endings, I just could not devise an outcome which brought me comfort. I tried prayer but felt that I was being told in return something like "Ye reap what ye sow" and "How can you have the brass neck to come crawling now?" I couldn't disagree. Finally, the alarm came as an unlikely welcome friend.

It was a relief to be driving over seventy-five miles to

work early in the morning as I counted down the minutes until I could make the call. Each of my clocks informed me that it was 8am, and as I pressed the number on my car phone, I felt my heart resting uncomfortably in my mouth.

"Hello, Causeway, blah blah blah blah." I couldn't make out a word being said.

"Hello, my name is Colin Campbell and I received a call last night asking me to phone today." I was doing my best to be calm while suppressing the desire to scream out loud. I was eventually referred to someone else, as the gentleman who had left the message for me was on leave. Very considerate of him to take a holiday after delivering that bombshell. Eventually, I was informed that the doctor wanted me to come in to have a bronchoscopy something or other, but I was still no wiser as to what was to become of me. When I asked how serious this was, the guy, understandably, mentioned that it was for the doctor to discuss with me, and if he had been an American, he probably would have said it was above his pay grade. I then came up with a cunning ploy. As casually as I could, I mentioned that I was heading off for a skiing holiday and would appreciate confirmation from the doctor that it would be safe for me to do so.

"It has cost a few bob to arrange, and I might need the doctor's help to get it back through the insurance," I ventured. It appeared casually brave, nonchalant even, to be focusing on a few hundred pounds when I was actually frightened that my life was over. The response was as if I hadn't spoken at all. There wasn't one. I pushed it further by asking if she was available, and while I am sure he genuinely made an effort, he confirmed that she was not free, but as if anticipating that I was about to become awkward – and I was – he offered to have her call me as soon as she had a moment, which would probably be between 12 and 1pm. *Today, that is?* I thought it but said nothing, as following his assurance that she would indeed speak with me, I ended the call feeling a little better, if only because I had done something rather than submissively done nothing and hoped for things to happen on my behalf.

I told the chairperson of the meeting I had driven to Belfast to attend that I might need to leave without prior notice to take a call, using my expression as an indication as to the gravity of the subject matter, and I waited. And waited. And waited. I was nearly back to my car to make the homeward journey when my phone rang.

"Is that Mr Campbell?" a voice asked.

"Yes," I replied, as now was not the time for one of my typically more expansive but unfunny responses.

"I have been asked to call you about your last scan."

I was about to 'explain' about my impending holiday and concerns about skiing when it all came gushing out. "Do I have lung cancer? Am I going to die?" I was standing in the middle of the street asking this question, with people walking by on either side of me.

Her answer was priceless, "I don't think we need to go there just yet." *Just yet...? Just what? Just when?*

"Will I be able to ski?" As if that even mattered, given my previous outburst.

"We noticed something in the scan and would like

to do a bronchoscopy with you when you get back." That sounded a whole lot better.

I went on the skiing holiday, the worst part of which was the skiing, and upon my return the broncho thing took place, although I can barely remember anything about it. Only a couple of weeks' later I received official confirmation that what they had seen in the scan was no reason for concern and I would only need further check-ups every so often. I had come through my scare, but the experience made me determined that for the rest of my life I would never take anything for granted and would be ready to deal with whatever was thrown at me. And, of course, I meant it.

1

"We looked at your X-ray and unfortunately we discovered a lesion in the liver."

The consultant spoke slowly and politely in that noncommittal way which suggested that he understood the effect of his words but knew from experience that there was no easier way to deliver such a heartbreaking message. Deidre smiled and nodded, while clearly trying to take in what was happening.

"Is there anything else, Doctor?"

There was a barely discernible pause. He seemed to be able to breathe in while continuing to talk. "The scan highlights a growth in the breast, which is the primary cancer, and it has spread to the liver." Have you ever been punched very, very hard while trying to stay on your feet? "It is also in the lung." And then you are floored.

"What does all this mean?" Deidre asked, maintaining her composure despite the plane crash which her life had suddenly become, obviously hoping for even a glimmer of something that could in any way be interpreted as good news.

1

"We will make an appointment for you with the breast specialist on Monday, and he will be in a better place to advise of treatments and the way forward."

"Is this terminal?" Deidre asked, as if enquiring whether something was available in the sale. When the consultant did not answer immediately, she changed her tone, and a hint of desperation surfaced. "Can you tell me anything? Anything positive?"

"You will need to speak with the breast specialist. I deal with bowel complaints, but he will be able to go through the options with you on Monday." So that was that then.

Me? I had frozen. I was known as someone who was never lost for words, but words right now were as useless as some people think they always are. Right now it didn't really matter anyway, because I had none. Right now I was looking at my partner but not actually seeing her and struggling with what to think next, what to say, and what to do. Here it was, a nightmare from which there would be no waking up.

On 24 January 2020, at 2.10pm. It was at that moment when we looked at each other, and without saying anything, we knew our lives would never be the same again. Even though the relevant thoughts had not developed and the consultant's words had not yet delivered their full impact in my head, something inside, something instinctive, knew. Just knew. As if reading my mind, Deidre said, "This is the end of our life as we know it."

Only two hours ago I had been discussing where to place the apostrophe at the end of a word to differentiate between the genitive singular and genitive plural, as in

2

doctor's and doctors'. As if it mattered. Well, it did matter then, and probably it will again if we ever find a way back to normality. But not just now.

Friday at 2.22pm. It's strange how you notice seemingly irrelevant details at times like this, at the exact time when, in the space of barely more than ten minutes, it felt like everything had come to an end. The consultant had been very accommodating and empathetic in agreeing to meet. Deidre had received an initial call just after 12pm that day, telling her she had been given an appointment for the following Monday, but after reflecting on the certainty of a weekend consumed by anticipation and worry had called back to ask if she could speak with someone now, as she did not want to have to wait for three more days. Although the consultant was not officially working, he was at his office and agreed not to make her wait until Monday if she could come at 2pm and be accompanied. He added that the news was, to quote, "Not good."

When Deidre called and relayed the message, the creeping fear that had begun to gnaw at me following her first call became a full-on charge. Totally out of keeping with her medical history, she had been in severe pain for most of the previous week, leading us to think that she must be suffering from something like gall bladder or some other non-life-threatening condition. But now that worry, the one which causes physical reactions such as dry mouth, rapid heartbeat and perspiration, was developing into fear of something truly unthinkable. Why, otherwise, would the doctor be delivering the message like this? I left my own place of work right away and, fearing the

3

worst for the first time, became so consumed by negative thoughts that I could not recall the journey home. When I arrived, it was a case of there being nothing to say, and yet, at the same time, everything to say. We did not speak as we drove to the hospital. Luckily, today we had both been working close to home, and as the hospital was nearby, we would be spared a long drive. I was thankful for that, as it was like no other journey I had undertaken. Nothing, but nothing, prepares you for this.

I was only the partner, and the diagnosis was not mine, but the hammer blow it delivered was more intense than anything I had ever felt in my life; and I have known heartbreak and failure. We were totally unprepared. Even those with no direct personal experience will probably have known someone who has been through this kind of diagnosis and will have been sympathetic, wishing them all the best and then, quite understandably, refocusing on what is for dinner or on television that night. We are not bad people for doing so, as it is a built-in psychological mechanism to protect us from absorbing constant pain coming from the world around us, helping us to get on with our own lives as well as possible on a daily basis. This is as it should be. It is nothing to be ashamed of, and I have been there several times with friends and acquaintances. But when the news arrives at your own door, it is different. So different. I think we were both left numbed and unable to take in what we had heard, and I could only look at my partner, and along with a strong feeling of love for her came an overwhelming sense of utter helplessness.

How we made it back from the hospital, I will never know, because I certainly cannot remember any part of that journey either. Yet, once home, we seemed to find ourselves sitting in the hall without consciously deciding to do so. Now here I was looking at this small, vulnerable person with whom I had been sharing my life, this person I had fancied from afar, pursued, won, nearly lost, nearly lost again, become engaged to, feared was going to leave me and for whom now all I felt was one massive, all-consuming wave of pure, unconditional love, and as my sense of helplessness began to recede, I felt a determination to do something – anything – to save her. Nothing else in life mattered. We sat for what felt like an hour but was probably no more than a few minutes, and almost as if we were rehearsing for a scene from a play, Deidre, thankfully, cleared her throat and spoke first.

"We will fight this," she said through light tears.

"And we will win," I responded, clenching my fist and pumping it as if a goal had been scored.

"You know what? Let's do all the things we want to do and worry about nothing else any more!" The fact that this was so unlike her added more poignancy and pain to the acclamation.

"We can do that okay," I affirmed, sensing a more positive atmosphere than I had feared.

"Everything we have always wanted to do, we will do."

I paused, strangely enthused, given the circumstances, by what I was hearing.

"I love you so much," she said.

"And I love you so much too," was the easiest, most obvious, response I have ever had to make in my life.

"I wish I had told you that more often," she half whispered as she embraced me like never before.

"Don't worry now, honey. We have probably taken each other for granted a little, but not from now on..." was, again, the easiest of replies.

"From now on," she continued. "From now on we will go where we want, we will not worry about money, we will not worry about anything. Life is too precious and time is too short for that."

I agreed wholeheartedly, and I would have agreed enthusiastically with anything she suggested, at least I thought I would. It was a strange feeling, but despite the earth-shattering news we had just received – and at this time we had no idea whether she would live for a day, a week, a month, a year, or beyond – we appeared to be hit with a delirious wave of optimism. Not at all what I had expected coming back from the hospital. It was as if we had been drugged or hypnotised, as if in some perverse sense we had realised that we had been relieved of all the relatively minor worries and irritations of the world because we now had something truly life-threatening to occupy us.

Whatever it was – and I still do not fully understand it – it carried us through the early moments of shock. And I now realise that it is possible to laugh and cry at the same time. Having flown the skies – business class of course – and sailed the oceans in luxury sea liners – Cunard, naturally – in our new narrative, it was inevitable that our focus would shift from travel, but I could never have anticipated our next planned acquisition.

"You know what? Let's get a dog," Deidre proclaimed as she built upon her own momentum.

"Yes, let's," I replied, the words leaving my mouth, but not without a fight.

Let's what? I thought. *Get a dog? Good God, a dog? Me, the most allergic person on earth. Oh please, God. Anything but a dog. I could even suffer tickets for Rod Stewart, but not a dog. I can't even breathe when the Paul O'Grady show comes on TV. Even Scooby Doo makes me wheezy.*

"It can be one of those hypo-allergenic ones… a wee Shih Tzu… like Mummy's." As if the thought of another dog like Mummy's was going to sell it to me. "You'll love it. I know you will."

I won't, but already I know I'm going to lose this one.

"Yes, of course, honey. We can look into that soon enough, when we get sorted." To be honest, I would have acquired the Loch Ness Monster had she asked me to.

Now was not the time to challenge anything she was saying, as I needed this wave of positivism to sustain us for as long as possible, and at least until I knew what to say and do for the next period of time, so that we could gain some idea as to what the longer term plan needed to be. With Monday only a few days away, and with all its possible bombshells to go off, we had to find a way of getting through Friday night, Saturday and Sunday. Somehow. Then we could get on with sorting everything else out. And with a little Shih Tzu on the way, we were obviously getting sorted much more speedily than I expected.

Then, for the first time since we returned to the house, I noticed that we had become silent, and it appeared that Deidre might be settling back for a doze. How wonderful that would be. I watched her eyes close and her shoulders slump a little in her chair as she took on the breathing pattern of someone falling into a sleep. With my own mind beginning to wander, and exhaustion setting in, I descended into darkness, reflecting on events that had made up the lifetime that had been the past week and 17 January 2020.

"I have a terrible pain in my side."

"That's all the badness trying to get out," was my typical, less-than-helpful reply.

"No, seriously."

In all the years I had known this person, she had been sick for two days at most, so clearly something was not as it should be.

"I remember you mentioning something about your side when we were taking the Christmas tree down, and I had warned you to take it easy." That was obviously it; she had pulled a muscle or something in the annual tree-dismantling ritual.

"It's not that. It's terrible."

It clearly was by the sound of her voice, and within forty minutes we were in the quieter than anticipated Sunday-morning Accident and Emergency ward at the local hospital in Ebrington, on the outskirts of the city of Derry/Londonderry, whichever tickles your fancy.

A & E, as we call it, was dank, cold and soulless, with stories of hangovers from alcohol or drugs, injuries from fights, and despair written all over the faces of many of this morning's clients. I tend to consider myself a man of the world, but places like this remind me of how little I have seen of the other side of life – the emptiness, sadness, hopelessness, the apparent lack of something to live for except the next fix or fight. But this morning my emotion was of pity, not disgust. That, and concern for Deidre.

To think that kids study for years to become doctors in order to work in a place like this. The Health Service has numerous critics, but I am not one of them. I acknowledge that many people do not receive the service they need when they need it, and perhaps, as I have been fortunate to have had my conditions treated quickly and properly, I have expected similar to happen for everyone. Despite that, A & E would never rank among my favourite places to spend time. Thankfully, on this occasion, we were seen to quickly.

After receiving assurances that she was beginning to feel better already, and Conan, the elder of the two boys, who had been visiting for the weekend from Belfast with his wife, Suzanne, would be able to collect her, I convinced myself that there was nothing more I could contribute, so I left to make my weekly Sunday journey to take my eighty-seven-year-old mother for lunch.

I was relieved because I knew how much my mum looked forward to my visits, short and sweet as they were. As I had managed to make up time on the largely deserted roads, I did not even have to apologise for being late; as with many people of her generation, if you were to tell my mum you would be there at 1.15, 2.17 or 3.19, that would be the time she would expect you at the door, and as she had never driven a car, the old traffic jam story did not carry any weight and was not worth attempting. I decided to mention nothing of the morning's events, not wishing to worry her unnecessarily, because we all know how mums like to have a good worry. And anyway, there was nothing really to report. Lunch with my mum would pass as lunch with my mum always passed.

"How are you, Mum?" I begin as cheerily as possible, despite what I am anticipating.

"Well, I'm not 100%, Son. You know how it is. I've been running a bit again at night and my knee is sore. But sure, you've just got to get on with it, haven't you?" I am not wrong.

"Yes, Mum. Mum, you're eighty-seven years old, remember, so what do you expect? None of us is 100% any more. I'm sixty-one, and I'm not 100% either. You are very fortunate to be in such good health overall. Aren't you, Mum?"

Unfortunately, these attempts to deliver a motivational speech never came across as intended – to encourage her to rejoice in how fortunate she is and ignore the odd ache and pain. No matter how I try, my frustration surfaces, and it sounds more like a telling off to a vulnerable adult from an uncaring son.

"Yes, I suppose, when you think of what some people have to live with, I'm very lucky." she states without an ounce of conviction in order to close this particular transaction, as mums do. But never, as it became clear to us the following week, were truer words spoken.

We would go to the same restaurant at the same time to sit at the same table and, in my case, to eat the same meal – fish – because I always want to leave space for my real Sunday dinner, usually a roast, later that evening with Deidre and any family who happen to be there for the weekend. My mum provides me with an update on who has died, her friends who are still here, the weather, the bin man and the biscuits she buys him for returning her bin to the back of the house, and the various fraudsters who have called during the week trying to separate her from her money. I could write the script, but I don't mind; it works, and it helps. I am occupying my mum's world for those few hours, and that is in no bad thing. She has been a wonderful mother and friend through the years, and I love her dearly, even if there are times when I could run far away.

Unfortunately, even in polite company, I have inherited her trait of eating quickly, and once I set my knife and fork down after finishing my food, we complete the final part of the ritual when she asks a waitress, all of whom are shining lights of serenity and patience, for a box to take the half of her meal which she not eaten home with her. I will pay the bill – with her money, as she insists it is her treat – and then bring the car round to the front door of the restaurant to collect her. It's only when I see her emerge from the doorway coming towards the car that I fully realise how much she has aged. When I see her like that, memories come flooding back – all happy – and more often than not, I feel the urge to cry.

On the short journey back to her house – it is not the

house we grew up in, therefore, to me, it is not home – she will perform another ritual which is, "Are you in a hurry home, Son?"

As I know what is coming, I am able to cut to the chase, "Why, Mum? Is there anything you need?"

"It's just if you have time, Son, maybe we could call into Tesco for some ham and ribs."

"When do you need them for, Mum?" Not that it matters, as I am going to do it anyway.

"Well, it's just that I may not get down during the week, and I like to have stuff just in case."

I force a laugh and continue, as we have not reached the shops yet,

"Mum, there is stuff falling out of your fridge, so in case of what?" I am more than happy to oblige, although this week, for the first time, I was anxious to get home as soon as I could. I do my mum's shopping every week, usually on the Saturday, and take it with me the following day. This arrangement enables me to complete the exercise quickly, whereas, as I am about to experience yet again, when my mum goes into a supermarket, we are fortunate to ever come out alive. I leave her at the main door of the supermarket, park the car and then try to find her, as, inevitably, she has wandered.

Once we have captured the ribs, ham and several other items she magically remembers she might need, we head for home, after the final exercise of finding the car and getting it back to the main door to collect her has been completed. Sunday afternoon shopping, with its legions of the haunted and hung-over, is not for me.

We sit in her house, me with a cup of coffee and two buns I won't eat, and she with a cup of tea and two buns she will eat, until she is assured that the television will not mysteriously break down and she gets to saying, "Well, Son, I don't want to keep you, with that long journey home. Where is it you're going to again?" I usually make a play of futile resistance, but on this occasion, it's a quick hug and I am away with all the speed of a frightened rabbit. As I started up the car and pulled off the kerb while thinking of Deidre, I repeated to myself that there was nothing to be worried about.

To shorten the journey, I usually have the radio on, with either 'Sounds of the Seventies' on BBC Radio 2 or a football commentary, but on this occasion, although the radio was on, I was not hearing anything. I instead reverted to repeating the mantra that there was absolutely nothing to worry about. It continued to be answered by a question: *In that case, why are you so anxious to get home?* I made no response.

When I arrived, Deidre reported the official verdict that her pain was caused by an inflamed gall bladder, which seemed feasible to us all, and which could probably be treated with tablets or, perhaps, light surgery, but to be on the safe side, they asked for a scan to be carried out on the Tuesday morning. Nothing too sinister then. We had an enjoyable meal, a glass or two of wine and wished Conan and Suzanne well on their drive home. Onward to Tuesday.

I had a dental appointment scheduled for that morning at a practice nearby, meaning I would be a little bit late for work, but I was not concerned, as I would easily make the time up and I had an understanding boss. As it turned out, being close to home was fortuitous for another reason. I had heard my phone vibrate in my overcoat pocket when I was in the dentist's chair and assumed it would be a work issue, something that would have to wait until my release. I don't mind a visit to the dentist and regularly fall asleep in the chair, regardless of the tortures they are visiting upon me. The greatest torture of all is, of course, settling the exorbitant bill, particularly as I often appear to be the only one who actually has to pay for their treatment. I had a quick glance at my phone on the way back to the car. Deidre… Two missed calls. *That's unusual*, I thought, but that night's tea was a much-considered subject for discussion, so that would be it. I returned the call, and as it connected, and without a word being spoken, I just knew.

"Colin, can you take me to hospital? I'm not feeling too good at all, and I don't feel like driving. Can you take me?"

I responded immediately in the affirmative, which, for a few seconds, took my mind off what could possibly be happening.

"I take it it's your gall bladder?" I asked hopefully but could not disguise the doubtful tone in my voice, "No problem. Of course. I'll be there in under ten minutes, and there is nothing to worry about." As I turned on the ignition and moved off, worry was exactly what I was feeling.

When I pulled into the driveway, Deidre did not look any different from when I had left her in the morning.

I am not sure what I was expecting to see, but I took encouragement from that fact. We arrived at the hospital, and without any undue delay she had the scans taken. All we could then do was wait. But only until Friday, 24 January, as it turned out.

We can spend many days of our lives waiting for results – exams, sports, job interviews or other applications, and medical scans. No matter what we do in the time between the scan and the result, no matter how meaningful our activities, they will be simply a series of distractions, killing time. Such a sinister term. We cannot kill time, but we can waste it.

I have been complimented in the past for my patience and my ability to wait for my turn. Probably, some of it is inherent, while the greater portion may well have come from training and life experiences. In any event, I am sure a similar acknowledgement has never been passed in Deidre's direction, as she wondered aloud how long it would take before she heard and whether she should phone them. We agreed, however, to wait, as calling might, in some way, annoy them. At least I had experience of this particular waiting game and knew we did not want to hear anything too soon.

"They have so many to get through, it could be a couple of weeks at least, so let's just relax and put it out of our minds," I reasoned. Who was I convincing?

Despite the open-plan layout in my workplace, it is possible to find a small meeting room with privacy, and thankfully my colleague and I were in one of these rooms when my mobile rang on the Friday morning shortly after twelve. If you are able to sense what a result is going to be before hearing it, you will know how I was feeling. The conversations took place, I took my leave and our lives changed forever.

We seemed to awaken from our doze at the same time, and my reflections on the past week were over, and we busied ourselves with changing clothes and preparing for dinner. The mood was slightly different, less excited, but neither of us had the energy to engage in any deep conversation, so avoidance was the best approach. The time passed slowly, but we both managed to eat and watch TV.

Our next challenge was to go to bed and try to get some sleep. As a child, I used to wonder why we go to bed when we do not need to, when we are not tired, when it seems like the last place on earth we should possibly be? As an adult, despite being constantly tired, I still rarely sleep when I get there. But we continue to go to bed, concerned about getting our eight hours. Convention has much to answer for at times.

I lay awake, listening for everything, a movement, a sniffle or hopefully even the sound of someone sleeping. I was also ready to talk if Deidre wanted to, but in all honesty I was frightened, as I had no idea what to say. Finally, hearing nothing, tiredness did kick in, and I found myself starting to drift into darkness and about to fall into a thick nothingness. Drifting, drifting until I could hear a voice in the distance, soft at first but increasing in volume, indistinguishable when it was accompanied by a shaking sensation until I woke with the realisation that my partner was upset. I froze involuntarily, unable to think of something to say, something to do.

"Please," I said to myself, or to some higher power who might happen to be listening. Meaningless perhaps, but I needed something.

"I'm sorry," she replied heartbreakingly.

I was feeling sick with panic, and as that returning sense of uselessness was becoming overwhelming, something came to me. I cleared my throat, as this would have to be good. "I remember that many years ago I was told that in my darkest moments I should say the words 'the Lord Jesus Christ' over and over again until I calmed down and lost the fear."

No reaction *Why did I have to say that? Is that it? Is that all I've got? Useless. I can't do this. What will I do? Please, God, what can I do?*

I tensed up and waited, fearing a verbal rebuke, but instead silence, and then her voice. "What was it again?"

"The Lord Jesus Christ, over and over again." I waited, with my heart pounding like a bass drum at a disco but trying not to breathe or cause any distraction. Eventually, brilliantly, I recognised the soft, short breaths of my partner sleeping and at rest.

"Thank you, Lord," I whispered to myself and Him for the first time in more years than I could remember as I also slipped off the cliff into the abyss.

2

The next morning, Saturday 25th, did not start well. Although we both appeared to wake from our slumber at the same time, as always with this kind of sleep, we were neither rested nor refreshed. Understandable, but I was relieved that we woke together, as I did not want Deidre to be alone with her reflections on the previous day for even one second, and as if she were thinking the same thing, we immediately resumed talking, realising that any period of silence may well bring the impact of what had happened into even greater focus.

Despite our best efforts, however, she had obviously processed more of what had been said the day before, and with a revised perspective affecting her emotions, things deteriorated further. In an effort to lift the mood, I decided it was time to resume the lottery-winning-type fantasies: all the things we were going to do, all the opportunities we were going to take, all the money we were going to spend.

We rose and continued to converse, despite it being clear that Deidre had already begun running down her mental to-do list, and while quite obviously in shock, she appeared to be thinking through the actions which required her immediate attention in a calm, objective manner, true, as always, to her style of handling matters when under pressure, something I was grateful for right now. She had already called her brother and sister-in law, who were obviously stunned at the news, but the warmth of their reaction was a comfort to her. She sat in silence for a few minutes, then suddenly, "I need to tell the boys and Suzanne. I will tell Conan first, as he is near, but I am worried about Aidan, as he is over there on his own. He will be upset and want to come home. I will wait and see what Conan thinks."

"Good idea," was all I could say, but as I sat back in my chair, my concern was that she would take on too much trying to let everyone know before we even knew ourselves. I did not want her to exhaust herself, because somehow we had to get through to Monday.

I imagine most people have experienced a time when they pondered what they would do when faced with a life-or-death dilemma, where some kind of bravery and clear thinking was required in order to face up to the danger of the situation, similar in a way to any hypothetical scene, such as, if attacked by a robber, would you be a hero or run, 'fight or flight' as it is often referred to? For most of us, we will never know until the situation arises. I was frightened for Deidre. Frightened of what she would have to go through: the appointments, treatments, inevitable disappointments and pain. Most of all I was afraid of losing the love of my life. I tried to prevent this image from entering my mind, but I was not in control of my faculties, and it kept returning like a throbbing headache. There was nothing I could do to improve this catastrophe. How could I? I might be a trained counsellor, but I am no doctor, no way. I pondered while waiting for the kettle to boil. I needed to come up with something worthy of this lady. The steam rose, as the water had boiled, and I poured my first coffee of the morning. We would beat this. Somehow.

From childhood I had been mesmerised by heroes of the silver screen and, unusually for someone from Belfast at that time, in particular American super heroes in masks and capes; and as often as I could afford it, I would take the bus to Smithfield Market in Belfast, where a few shops sold those comics. What a den of hidden treasures Smithfield was! Then there was watching James Bond at the Park Picture House on Oldpark Road in Belfast with my dad when I could not have been more than eight or nine years old – I am not sure what the age ratings were for Bond movies at that time – watching four screenings of the first Tim Burton *Batman* movie in the one day; the *X-Men* comics long before the movies appeared; the John Wayne and Randolph Scott westerns which were my grandfather's favourites; Clint Eastwood's brooding menace to modern-day anti-heroes, mostly shaven headed and less overtly glamorous. They all feed our need to believe that we can do something good, even in the worst of circumstances, be it save the planet, the day, or at least the damsel in distress. Now my very own damsel was in severe distress, and where was I? Reality does bite eventually. The knowledge that no loaded gun nor special car, dark mask nor colourful cape, starry badge nor martial art can battle against the utter sense of powerlessness you feel when your partner is sitting in front of you with hope and positive thoughts disappearing like snow in the rain, is a cold, dark reality call. I imagined soldiers in a trench, waiting for an enemy they know is out there and about to attack. Doubt, fear, loneliness, knowing something terrible is going to happen but unsure as to when.

If this is how I was feeling, how must my partner be faring? How could she possibly be handling all of this devastating news? She could never have seen this coming. I appreciate no one does, but she had never darkened a doctor's doorway since I had known her, and in all of our time together appeared to be in bristling good health. Now she was dealing with shock and fear. Fear of the future with endless appointments and, if she was lucky, ongoing treatments, and having to live with the effects of chemotherapy. Fear of not being able to fulfil her dreams for herself and her family. Fear of not seeing her grandchildren. Fear of it all being over before her time. Fear of losing hope. Fear of dying.

I thought of my own father and how I could have used his help now. He'd always seemed to have an answer when it came to being a good person. There was not a day passed when I did not think of him nor miss him. Reflecting on all of this, I decided that whatever it was I had, I was determined to use it to help her in any way I could, doing whatever she needed. Nothing less.

One thing I did know, however, was that she had not been at all looking forward to telling the boys. The phone call was made late morning, and Conan, naturally, was overcome with shock and broke down in tears. I took no part in the conversation, as it had to be between the two of them because our mum is the one person we all need most, and, sadly, the person we tend to take most for granted. She is always there to provide, listen and make things right. That anything could possibly go wrong with our mum is unthinkable.

Deidre's relationship with her sons is excellent, and once Conan had collected himself, regardless of how he was really feeling, he appeared to be taking it in his stride, saying the right things, which calmed and assured his mum. Shock is such that we never know how we will react in frightening situations until we are faced with them. How are children of any age meant to react when they hear such news? Thankfully, in his case, well, as despite the diagnosis, we immediately came to an unspoken agreement that no matter what the odds, his mum would make it. She always did. His response was, therefore, everything we needed, and helped build the shelter of calm we were trying to erect around us. I was relieved by his reaction, a positive first tick in the notification of family and friends to-do list. He has always been a great kid, and I had quickly grown to love him and his wife dearly. I was confident they felt similarly about me too.

Before ending the call, they insisted on coming up to us, and I was delighted, as awaiting their arrival would be a welcome distraction. Our afternoon snack received as much attention to detail as most wedding receptions, but it was worthwhile because it kept Deidre occupied in the same way the bereaved insist on serving endless sandwiches and cups or tea before and after the funeral service.

When the doorbell rang, Deidre asked me to answer, even though she knew it was them and she was usually the first point of contact. While they had visited only recently, under totally different circumstances, it was great to see them, and they disguised their upset well with assurances based on their experiences of other people's parents. We are all prone to the 'I know someone who...' phenomenon, but when there is a happy ending, it does help.

We decided to go out for a meal, agreeing that it would be good to get a change of scenery and to lighten the atmosphere, which had intensified as we ran out of things to say that weren't about the diagnosis. We chose a casual dining restaurant in the city run by two local lads where we had previously been during weekdays and early on Saturdays, when it was not too busy, and we thought it would be a good idea to go there to get out and face the world. It boasted good food with a well-paced service, and the relaxed atmosphere would meet our requirements. *What a wonderful idea. We will go out and enjoy ourselves as if nothing is wrong. This can be done. A great idea. The best idea in the world! Yes!* As we had not booked early enough, our reservation was for later in the evening than on previous occasions, so when we arrived, it was busy. Very busy. I knew it was a wrong decision within about thirty seconds. Previously, we had been able to go straight to our table, which provided us with plenty of room in our immediate surroundings, and space was something we needed on this occasion. But now we had to wait for about ten minutes, and while normally that would not have been a problem, this time it was little short of a disaster. The lady, who knows us and usually fixes us up with a decent table, was doing her best to sort something out, all the while oblivious to our new circumstances. I expressed my gratitude to her, hoping that in some way it would speed things up, but seeing the obvious distress on Deidre's face, with people spilling past her from all angles, I did not know what to do for the best, whether to try to persuade her to leave and risk making a fuss, or act as if nothing was wrong and hope we'd get through.

Having asked her if she was okay a couple of times and receiving an affirmative but unconvincing nod, I did not know whether to accept her assurance in the hope that we would have the meal or take matters into my own hands, take us home immediately and accept that the project had gone badly wrong. Although I failed to make a call, paralysed by ifs and buts, it turned out that having consulted with Deidre one more time, to her increasing irritation, we stayed for the meal at her insistence and left immediately afterwards. I know she spent the whole time miserable, as the noise and close proximity of so many people were too much for her, while I was angry with myself for not taking better control of the situation. Never have I been so glad to leave a restaurant.

We made the return journey in silence. The night was not only unsuccessful but counterproductive, as it fuelled our fear that Deidre would be unable to enjoy something as simple as going out for dinner, one of our favourite activities. When we finally made it home, Conan and I, frustrated, blamed the lateness of the reservation and how the restaurant was too crowded, although we should have known, as it was Saturday night, for heaven's sake. I used the discussion to press home the message that we would continue to go out regularly in the future. After all, we had many weeks, months and years ahead for great nights out by ourselves, and with our family and friends.

The experience had come about much too soon after her diagnosis, but, equally, staying at home in a panic was no solution either. And in agreeing to go, Deidre had been trying to manage the situation despite the immense shock. She wanted to assure us that she was coping, but underneath it all, understandably, she was unable to take the whole thing in. I should have realised this but was in a hurry to make everything seem like Conan and Suzanne had nothing to worry about.

My mind, tiring, mulled over how badly it had all gone. *This was a terrible idea. The worst idea in the world. What was I thinking? Get your act together!* Nothing more was said on the issue, and I committed to keeping a closer eye on Deidre to try to better understand how she was faring. I knew there could be no more failures.

That night, as I lay awake thinking, I hoped that as we progressed, the fear would become more manageable, and as she worked her way through her to-do list of people to notify, the repetition of her story would lessen the impact and she would somehow begin to relax. But how could anyone relax with this news, and how could any sane person – me – expect a sane person – her – to be able to relax? Truth was, I did not feel so sane at this time.

*

The following morning, as she continued through her checklist of things to do and people to contact, Deidre remembered her friend Joanne, who had been suffering from cancer for a few years, and decided to call her. Thankfully, they re-established their bond very quickly, and Joanne was able to provide practical advice, much of which Deidre was able to take on board immediately – nails, eyebrows and hair. I also knew Joanne and had always been very fond of her, and while her ongoing battle was no secret, after the initial shock upon hearing her news, its impact probably receded behind a clutter of other things in my mind. "That's terrible. I hope she pulls through. Now what's for dinner?" sadly can be a common reaction. Thankfully, consistent with the wonderful person she is, she was a delight, and her tips and general advice were greatly appreciated. When someone you love has cancer, it can feel like you are on the outside looking in – you are not the sufferer, so you cannot possibly understand – but Joanne was on the inside, and Deidre trusted her. She was speaking from ongoing personal experience, and that meant everything. There are times when you are reminded how wonderful people can be. Joanne, I love you.

At breakfast we found enough topics for discussion and avoided silence and cancer. But we knew what was coming later. I hoped that Conan's presence might make his mum's forthcoming discussion with Aidan less traumatic. I understood Deidre's initial reticence about breaking the news. He was on his own, away from family, in London, and as he is slightly more combustible than his elder brother – so is nearly everyone – she felt less able to predict his reaction. He had to be told; it was a no brainer, despite a mother's concern for her son all those miles away on his own. But Aidan has never let her down, and he wasn't going to now.

As I had to go to Belfast to see my mother – you already know how that will have passed – I missed the call, but when I returned home, I was relieved to see the three of them chatting over coffee, looking relaxed, so I guessed that all had gone well. After reacting to the news with understandable anguish, Aidan had recovered, as good people do, and by the end of their conversation was holding it together extremely well. And, I am told, he even thanked God that they had me with them. Even in the early days of this disaster, despite my own self-doubts, the positive things people were saying about me were of immense benefit, increasing my determination to come good. A small word of praise or gratitude can go a very long way, as if I needed reminding.

The atmosphere at dinner was subdued. We were all exhausted, and I think Conan and Suzanne were relieved to be heading for home. We were grateful also, as by now Deidre was drained and I had run out of positive things to say for one weekend and needed silence.

Before retiring, we discussed how we would tell our work colleagues that we would not be turning up in the morning, nor possibly any other morning. It wasn't about *what* to say, but about *how much* to say at this stage. We agreed that in our 'official announcement' to the world, we should keep to the main points, as we did not know the full story, so we drew up a statement with enough detail to respect people's integrity and their genuine care for us while, hopefully, not creating panic in our friends' and colleagues' circles. In any event, there were more difficult mountains to climb on Monday morning, and again, with that knowledge, we managed little if any sleep that night.

*

It was finally Monday, 27 January, and the morning meeting with the breast specialist. While it is impossible to meaningfully explain how we were feeling, I was as frightened as I could remember. I felt sick, and perspiration was seeping from my pores despite it being a cold, winter morning. As I anticipated the meeting, I worked my way through a range of possible outcomes, none of them good, and it reminded me that we could exert no influence whatsoever on the situation. Our lives were in the hands of people we had never even met. And, of course, this most destructive and horrible of diseases.

As we made our way to the hospital, a journey which could be measured in yards but seemed like hundreds of miles, we talked about how fortunate we were to have a cancer facility so close to home rather than in another city or some other faraway destination and agreed how terrible it must be for people who do not have this service on their doorstep. It had suddenly become relevant.

When we arrived, my first thought was to stay in the car park rather than face what was to come, but Deidre was the reason we were here, and she would need me to be focused, so I opened the car door, swung around, put my feet on the ground, left the car and hurried to the passenger door to assist her.

"I'm not gone yet," she said, but she knew I meant well and even managed a smile. I made a mental note to tell her at a more appropriate time how much that helped me.

The walk to the Cancer Centre was not comforted by my feet turning into lead weights, each taking a different direction. We could not have made less headway if we had been walking backwards, and I began to think of people through history who were made to walk to their deaths, through a street or on a plank, and it was no comfort at all. I even recalled the time I nearly drowned, possibly because, like now, I was struggling to breathe and keep my head above water. Now I felt I was drowning, but in a different pool. Deidre was silent, walking beside me, and I could only guess what she was going through. I held her hand, letting her know I was there for her, and whispered, "Time to focus." She heard me, and saying nothing in response, simply nodded. That was all I needed.

We entered the building with its dark atmosphere, subdued lighting and whispering clients. Thankfully, the medical team were on time and we did not have to wait any longer to learn our fate. The specialist confirmed the diagnosis and provided more detail. I think we were struggling to make sense of it all, particularly as I could not find any good news in his words. He looked quite young, although he was obviously highly competent, and he projected a confident and empathetic air while remaining ever so slightly distant. When you think about it, these guys could be breaking news like this on a daily basis, and the good ones are like a stage performer who has delivered the same lines for weeks but continues to convince the audience that the show has only ever been presented to them. He was managing our shock and disbelief sensitively without committing to anything or letting us put words in his mouth.

As he continued, his face began to go in and out of focus and his voice was coming and going as if I were very drunk or just about to fall asleep. But every word connected like another slice in a death by a thousand cuts. As Deidre sat there passively, outwardly looking calm, I was stuck to my chair. There was cancer in three areas of Deidre's body, possibly a fourth, but, again, he would leave that to someone else to confirm, this time the oncologist. The primary breast cancer had significantly spread to the liver and lungs. How in the name of God could this have happened? Each of them on their own sounded bad enough. How could it happen to someone so healthy and energetic? To someone so hardworking and honest? To someone so wonderful and so loved? It shouldn't happen to her. It shouldn't happen to anyone.

Last Friday morning we were looking forward to a dream trip to Ashford Castle, near Galway, at the end of this month. Now, only three days later, the dream was a nightmare which only seemed to be getting worse and leading to… I could not contemplate it.

Deidre asked when the cancer had first appeared but, worryingly, could not remember attending a breast-screening examination within the last few years, leading her to wonder aloud if she had not received an appointment notification, or, worse, had received one but failed to attend. Either option was unpleasant, as now was not the time for any form of recrimination. I could not imagine how she would react if the hospital had failed to notify her, but I wanted there to be a simple explanation, with no one to blame. The specialist, sensing a potential issue, despatched a nurse immediately in a low-key, nothing-is-wrong manner to find an answer. To everyone's relief, the nurse confirmed that Deidre had attended for a mammogram just on the deadline of the three years' cut off point. It was, therefore, plausible that she attended, nothing was diagnosed and the tumour had grown in the time immediately after that until now. In all this panic, this news actually brought some relief to us all. No one was to blame, and there could be no 'What if?' scenario.

When Deidre left the room for another scan, I could not contain myself.

"Please tell me straight, Mr…" – when you move above doctor level, you become Mister again, or so I am told – "do we have a chance at all here? Is there anything we can hope for?"

"Oh yes," he replied immediately, as if surprised to be asked despite the bombshells he had dropped. "With the right treatment programme, careful living and a bit of luck, she could look forward to many years yet."

I know what I felt like saying. I felt like saying, *Well, why didn't you tell her that when she was in the room? She needs something to hope for!* However, I did not. Instead I replied, "Thank you so much for saying that. It is such a relief, and we will do everything we can to help her." A chance. Somewhere in there, we had a chance.

At this point, with everything we had heard, I was ready to grab it, no matter how remote, with both hands. Despite this light in a very dark tunnel, which even now I cannot comprehend, I did not share this development with Deidre immediately. I did not want her to feel that any conversation had gone on behind her back, as if in some way I was being disloyal. Or because I did not want to build her hopes up. As she was already interpreting the specialist's and nurses' every word and body language, I thought this might only add to her confusion. It is difficult to look back without applying the rationale that even had I related what I had been told, it would have done nothing to lighten the atmosphere right at that time. Conscious decision or blind panic? I will never know for certain.

Waiting for Deidre in that room was like a snapshot of all that is good and bad about life's tapestry, as expert care, resources and medical advances were being pitched against disease, human weaknesses and fear. Women of all ages were dressed in similar pink gowns, many with head coverings, unintentionally making them look like extras from a medieval drama, and while the robes and coverings were absolutely necessary, they removed their individuality.

Each man, husband or partner, father or son, was patently uncomfortable, their body language highlighting the distress of someone who has no idea how to react, how to say, "I'm frightened too. I don't know what to do. I am meant to protect you but I am unable to and I am of no worth." If only they could say something like that, it would be a start. If only *I* could, I knew that would also help in our situation.

As each woman returned from the X-ray rooms, they sat with their partners, those who were accompanied, in silence as the men in the room, including me, were, as one, trying to deal with it all. When you are programmed to protect and defend, and when you cannot do either of these, frustration and anger can be the consequences. My grandfather on my mother's side was an absolute gentleman and treated my grandmother like a lady, like gold dust. The one thing he could not cope with, however, was any occasion when she was ill. It was as if he was angry at her for continuing to be sick even after a few cups of his tea and a large glass of Lucozade, an expensive drink in those days and used for medicinal purposes rather than to enhance sporting performance. As I grew older, I came to understand that his fear was of being unable to solve the problem, to protect her and save the day, because if he did not, he was not a real man. And when she was diagnosed with cancer in her early sixties, his fear of losing the only woman who was ever in his life was realised.

I could now say I understood, as I was sitting in a room full of men just like my grandfather, regardless of their age, with furrowed brows, looking at the floor, avoiding eye contact, but determined not to display any form of weakness. Well, believe me, we are all weak, we are all afraid, we are all human and we all fail from time to time. Looking around, discreetly, I sensed a room drowning in despair at what was happening and what was yet to come. And for many of us, despair is followed by resignation, exhaustion and acceptance of one's fate, that it was 'meant to be' and we could have done nothing to change it. Right then I made a commitment never to surrender to resignation but to encourage Deidre every step of the way. And if we were to achieve anything, we could only do it together. Experience has taught me the value of expressing and trying to understand my feelings, and I, therefore, felt a sense of warmth for the people, sufferers and their partners who have had to deal with this as if we now had a bond, a commitment to say, "I love you no matter what, and I am frightened and helpless too." That would do for now.

I will never forget that morning, particularly the young woman who broke down upon leaving the consultation room and appeared to have no one there to comfort her. While the nurse was skilled at consoling her, the news was obviously the worst it could be, and yet, despite knowing that watching her distress was only adding to the indignity of her experience, I could not draw my eyes away. Why was she alone? Did she not have a husband, a partner, a wife? A mum, dad, sister, brother, or even a friend? How could anyone be left to deal with this on their own?

As I finally diverted my gaze, it was clear that we were all doing our best, and if we knew how to do better, we would. But I wondered if any of our efforts would be enough. As if in response to my despair, I decided that this is a story which must be told, so that in some way it might be of some comfort to those suffering this most despicable of diseases and their loved ones. I promised myself that it would be my best ever effort.

I had no more time to dwell on my mission, as I was drawn back to this poor human being. Her cries were from the depths of her soul, and if despair made a sound, that would be it. I have seen death, and I have experienced serious accidents, but nothing sounded like this. I hope upon hope that she is still around today and recovering. Please be. You deserve it.

When Deidre appeared, so childlike and vulnerable, we exchanged only a few words, and it was clear from her demeanour that she needed to leave. We made it home in silence, but shortly after our arrival, she insisted that she wanted to call work, and I agreed that we should both do so, and we retired to separate rooms remembering what we had agreed to say.

Although my call to work had gone well, I had been apprehensive. I had to tell my colleagues about Deidre, which would be shock enough, and then of my own asthma condition, which had worsened, no doubt because of the shock. My boss and colleagues were taken aback by the news concerning both of us, and they told me to take as long as I needed to recover and asked me to pass my regards to Deidre and wished her all the best for the journey ahead. I knew I was lucky to have them, and I determined to stay in touch and meet them as often as I could over the weeks to come.

But for Deidre, it was worse, and I was worried, not only about how her colleagues might receive the news but of the possible effect on her, as by explaining what had happened, she would be confronted yet again with the cold reality of the situation. This was it. It was real. Someone who had been dedicated to her job and had given so much to it now had to tell her colleagues she was very sick and would be off for some time to come.

Most government workers remain in their respective jobs for only a few years before moving on to different if not necessarily greater things. That was certainly my experience. But Deidre was a very senior civil engineer within the professional and technical grades, as they were referred to in the civil service, where many staff could spend their entire careers within one relatively small network of colleagues, and that was the case with her, and in doing so she was fortunate. I believe she did not quite realise how lucky she had been to have worked with a group of people who had developed a bond of respect for their professional ethics, the jobs they were performing and for each other.

I did not know Deidre's colleagues well, the majority of whom were male, given her discipline, but from what I could surmise from my work-related discussions with her, they had a special relationship. And from her conversations with each of them, so it proved.

The calls were sequenced in accordance with the hierarchical line-management order, and each of her colleagues was shocked and concerned, and conveyed a deep sense of distress at the immediate loss, albeit temporarily we hoped, of a loved and valued team member and friend. They rallied round, those both junior and senior, and even the top civil servant in her department made contact to convey her concerns and best wishes.

She was clearly affected by the experience, but not quite in the way I had feared. Naturally, she must have sensed that her working life as she knew it was most likely over, and she could derive no comfort from that, but she was also impressed. Very, very impressed by how her colleagues responded and with the obvious high esteem and warmth in which they held her.

In her highly successful career, she had defied the odds and overcome challenges, and in doing so had won many admirers of her talent and dedication. And now their good wishes and warmth had given her an immense lift, and more than that, would sustain her in meeting the greatest of all challenges to come.

The rest of the evening passed without conversation, energy or appetite but with just a modest sliver of that thing we call hope. As far as I can recall, we slept that night.

3

On Tuesday, 28th, we started out on the 110-mile sojourn to Deidre's mum in Kilkeel, a journey I did not enjoy at the best of times with its town centre traffic hold-ups and endless winding roads. It was, however, imperative that we saw her urgently to break the news.

As we drove, I played through the various scenarios of how the encounter would unfold, as Deidre was concerned as to how her mum would react, but all we could do was tell her and take it from there. The only emotion stronger than worrying about a parent is surely that of worrying about a child. I had always had a very good relationship with Deidre's mum. I had called her to seek her permission before asking Deidre to become engaged all those years ago, and I know she appreciated my traditional approach. But now I was worried about both of them.

As my mind wandered, I thought about how we are all different; some throw hugs and kisses around like confetti, while others are more reserved, perhaps believing there is something undignified in such displays of affection. Deidre's mum, while tending towards the latter, had been a tremendous support to her through the years, especially when the boys were growing up, and she has never been found wanting. They have a very close, respectful relationship, and that is what matters. Deidre was a devoted daughter, frequently making the long journey to see her mum during the working week, and while she knew that it was not always necessary, as her mum seemed so self-sufficient, she always would. The forthcoming meeting would be like no other, but as it would simply take its course, I decided to keep driving and keep hoping.

When we entered Newry and its never-to-be-understood traffic junctions and one-way lanes, for the first time ever, although it had probably been there for years, Deidre noticed a shop which sold wigs, and remembering her conversation with Joanne asked me to turn back in order to pay a visit. I did not fancy the manoeuvre, but unbelievably the traffic vanished in front of us, and as we approached the shop, a parking space appeared right at the front door. Wonderful!

I had never thought much about what a wig shop would look like, as even though I had been head-shaving for years, a wig had never been on my to-do list. But when we went in, it was, unsurprisingly, full of wigs, so many styles and colours, female and male. When we were approached by a member of staff, my daydream ended,

"Can I be of any help?" she enquired in a warm and welcoming tone. Deidre began to speak but no words came out. I took a chance.

"My gorgeous partner, Deidre," I nodded towards her, with the member of staff doing likewise, "has just received a cancer diagnosis, and as we were passing and she wants to plan ahead, we thought we would pay a quick visit." The member of staff was used to these scenarios and skilfully eased our discomfort, enabling us to get on with our business.

She maintained her focus on Deidre, talking *to* her rather than *about* her, and once she understood what we wanted and where we were from, she provided some more good news by informing us that the owner of the business had a contract with Altnagelvin Hospital, where Deidre would be receiving her treatments, and would be able to get her fitted with whatever she wanted and have them delivered to the hospital in good time. She tried on a couple of incredibly realistic wigs and they made plans for the owner to make contact and take it from there. All in all, a positive experience.

As we continued our journey, after a period of silence Deidre spoke. "That went well, didn't it?"

"Absolutely." But I just wanted to cry. "The lady was lovely, and she certainly knew her stuff."

"Do you think the wigs look okay?" As if I was ever going to rain on this parade.

"They look superb, so realistic. In fact, they look like real hair," I exclaimed.

"They *are* real hair."

"Well, you know what I mean. They look great, and if you need one, you will look just as lovely as you are now."

"Thanks," she said softly.

"Thanks for what, honey?" I genuinely enquired.

"You know. Earlier. Thanks."

"That's okay. You don't need to worry about that. Any time." And now I could not resist a smile. I had been useful.

We have all witnessed how devastating cancer can be on the appearance. I hoped against hope that for Deidre the effects on her hair, nails, eyebrows and weight would be minimal. Our first experience went well. And the wigs did look good. But cancer not only attacks the vital organs; it also attacks the person's dignity, beginning with their looks, and I knew there was a long road ahead.

Our arrival at her mum's filled me with more trepidation than usual. I am highly allergic to her dog, Lucy, who sets off my asthma, but in the current situation, there was more to be apprehensive about. After the initial catch-up on who was doing what, Deidre explained that we had something to tell her and that I would do the talking. I had been prepared for this following our wig-shop experience. I delivered the news as clearly and concisely as I could, but as I was doing so, without planning to, I played down the seriousness of her diagnosis by not telling her the cancer had spread. I did not know why. Was I protecting her mother by softening the blow, or myself from having to say the words? There is never pleasure in delivering bad news. Nevertheless, the message was devastating.

In response, her mum said very little, probably trying to take it all in. No parent wants to hear news like that; it is not the natural order of things. Deidre's mum was not overly demonstrative in her manner, so her calm reaction was not out of character and was what we needed right now. For my part, I wondered if I had played down the severity of the diagnosis too much, but she asked no further questions, maintained her composure and for now my tactics appeared to have worked.

Tuesday evening in the local hotel in Kilkeel can be an underwhelming experience at the best of times, and on this occasion our mood was even lower than the atmosphere in the place. A quick main course, one drink and we were home before anyone would have noticed we had gone. The diagnosis was not discussed, and for this I was relieved because the last thing Deidre needed was to worry about how her mum was dealing with the news. Whether her reaction was an act of great strength or a facade to protect us, I could not decide, but I was grateful. Or maybe she instinctively knew I had not been completely forthcoming in my account. Once home, we all retired, but none of us slept a wink.

The following morning, after a light breakfast, we began the return journey, subdued. The three main family members had now been informed, and when we made it home, exhausted, we happily agreed not to speak to anyone for the rest of the day.

On Thursday we set off for Donegal to inform Deidre's Aunt Rose, a major player in the wider family circle. Many years ago, Deidre's mother bought a small thatched cottage situated on an inlet at Mulroy Bay, and across the road from Rose's and her late brother's house, enabling Deidre, who is now responsible for its upkeep, to take regular short idyllic holidays in that beautiful, rugged part of the county; and one of the pleasures of visiting is to meet Rose, her son and family, and whomever of the three daughters is visiting home at the time. She is the epitome of the aunt who could actually kill you with kindness, but it would be an incredibly pleasurable way to go. A homemade cakes, scones and buns heaven. Such is Deidre's regard for Rose and her family that she wanted to call with her so soon after the diagnosis.

While the usual preliminaries were observed, including tea and delightful scones, Rose, understandably, was clearly wondering why we were there in January when our earliest breaks were usually not until mid-May. I know she sensed something was wrong – people usually always do – and it was a relief when I was prompted to convey our terrible news. When I had finished, she remained as unflappable as ever and was just the person you would want to have on your side for the battles ahead. She was bound to have been shocked but said the right things in the right way. Deidre had a very good relationship with Rose, but until now I did not appreciate the extent. Thanks, Rose. We did not stay long, and after she undertook to inform the other family members in Dublin and all parts south, we took our leave, as there was nothing else to be said on this occasion and the experience had been wearing for all concerned.

On the way home Deidre disclosed that she was attempting to properly absorb her news and that as much as she tried not to be she was consumed with thoughts about her life expectancy. She described a recurring scene playing out in her mind as a series of car crashes, each one worse than the one before it, and much as she tried to look away, each time she saw that the victim's face was her own. All I could do was respond by saying that dreams of this kind were inevitable and understandable. I recalled my own scare from four years earlier and how fear of dying dominated my thoughts. As my torment had not lasted long, I concluded that talking about it now could be counterproductive, so I said nothing.

As our journey continued and we drifted into another period of silence, I began to reflect on why I had presented a more positive slant on Deidre's news to her mum and Rose. Positive bordering on unrealistic? I reasoned that saying the words out loud amplified how serious the situation was and that I was not ready to confront it. I then pondered whether my slant was to protect me rather than her mother and aunt. Perhaps none of us were ready to face up to the cold reality, ready to face up to what had happened. So, as yet, we didn't. There was work to be done, but for tonight, please God, let us sleep.

By Thursday, I had noticed that Deidre was eating less. She had been blessed with a healthy appetite, something we shared, so the change was concerning. I watched her rearrange the meagre amount of cereal in her bowl. "What's up?" I asked as if I had been on another planet for the past week.

"I'm just not hungry," was the reply, confirming the obvious.

"What do you think it is?" I enquired, ignoring the obvious, but I was trying. Silence. "What do you think it is?" I repeated, pressing the words home. "Well, is it mental, like you are worried, or are you sort of physically ill?" I knew what I meant but I was not explaining it well. I was petrified that, so soon, not eating would send her into severe decline. She confirmed that she was not hungry and was struggling with the news and, naturally, thinking about her life expectancy, reminding me that she had already told me that. Yes, she had, only last night. Hers was an understandable reaction, but that enlightenment did not help me come up with a useful response, "That's understandable, but I do not know how to react." When all else has failed, try the truth.

"Do I have days, weeks, months, years? I just don't know," she said. "Nobody knows," she added in a tone which intimated that the conversation was over.

"That's probably true, but we can do our best to make it lots of years, lots of happy years to come." And not a word of that was a lie.

"I am just frightened," came from someone so intensely private. Sometimes there simply are no words of comfort or inspiration.

"I know, darlin'. I'm frightened too." There, I had said it. We had both said it. She was frightened, and I was frightened of her dying. We spent the rest of the day catching up with some of the things we hadn't done for nearly a week, and attending to the basics was therapeutic. That evening we retired in peaceful silence knowing that enough had been said and that in some way we had made a step forward.

*

Psychologists talk about the reticular activating system, the part of the brain which sifts through the billions of pieces of information we absorb daily to identify those which are relevant to us. For example, if you are thinking of buying a silver car, you will suddenly be amazed at how many silver cars there are on the road, most of which you never noticed before. Similarly, if you take up a new hobby or interest, your world will quickly be filled with others who follow that pursuit, dedicated magazines, features in the media, and the like. It is a very efficient way of coming across helpful or interesting information, and I consciously use it quite often, particularly for police speed traps. It can, however, work in reverse.

I had been unaware of how many references there were to cancer in the various media until this week. It became apparent that once cancer had become relevant, mention of it could not be avoided. And on the Tuesday evening I even made the mistake of trying to change channel without being noticed.

"Did you turn over?" I was asked.

"Yes," I replied, honestly, as she had suspected that I had done it before.

"Why did you do that?" *I don't like where this is going.*

"I thought there was something I wanted to see on Four," I lied.

"Was it because it's about cancer?" I was cornered.

"Yes, honey, it was. I'm sorry." Sorry I was caught.

"You don't need to do that. It might be interesting."

"I just didn't know what to do, and I don't want you to be upset. That's all," I replied. This was true, particularly the bit about not knowing what to do. "If something comes on again, would you rather I just left it? I can do that." Little did I know.

Two hours later we sat down to watch a baking programme, the new rock 'n' roll, I am told. I was just coming to terms with wall-to-wall cooking programmes and now we had multiple baking series. Anyway, we watched, seeking some light relief, and as it was about baking cakes, nothing could go wrong. Nothing until the programme broke for the advertisements with the impossible-to-miss banner stating in all its glory, "Stand up to cancer!" *But I won't be turning over!* When the programme returned, they ran a feature on a young man who had obviously had cancer, and when he was interviewed, he looked so good that I felt the need to comment on his healthy appearance implying that it was a sign that all would be good for us too. As his story developed, however, the next footage of him highlighted a marked deterioration, with the commentator confirming that his treatments were no longer working. This was obviously a tragedy for the man and his family, but it was also a shock for us in our circumstances, desperately seeking anything encouraging to hold on to. A caption then appeared stating that the man had subsequently passed away, which left us quiet, and me unsure how to react.

"Every situation is different, and that need not be us," I finally offered, feeling the need to say something. I knew my tone was less than convincing, but the words were out of my mouth before I could think it all through.

"Absolutely. It's terrible for that young man and his family, but it has no bearing on my cancer." I resisted the urge to cheer, as this was better than I could have hoped for. I said nothing and she continued, "It depends on the type of cancer, and his was different to mine." Okay, that would do for now. Now, if only I could turn my reticular activating system off, I might get some sleep.

*

By Friday, 31 January, we had survived the lifetime that was our first week. And week two started well. Another nugget of advice from Joanne, her fellow metastatic-breast-cancer sufferer and good friend, to Deidre was to arrange to have her eyebrows bladed because they, along with most of her other hair, might fall out. This process needed to be done urgently, as Joanne confirmed that the hospital would be likely to refuse permission once her treatments began. I did not know why that might be, but I had never had my eyebrows bladed, so, while not understanding what was going to happen, I responded with enthusiasm at the prospect. There was excitement in her voice as we arrived at the salon across the city, and I downed endless mugs of coffee as I waited to collect her. I did not feel like being home alone.

It was a success; she was delighted with the results. The beautician, it transpired, had dealt with people in her position before. After the treatment we went for coffee – yes, more coffee – and Deidre confided that she was gaining strength from finding out about the wonderful people who were also going through their own diagnoses, helping her realise that she was not alone. Here was a whole new group of people who were living their lives and were being strong, open and friendly with their fellow sufferers.

A camaraderie similar to that with her work colleagues and friends. Then after a period of silence – I learnt from then on to keep talking – we came back to life expectancy, and the mood changed. I did not want to lose the warmth of the morning so far and decided to take a risk, "Darling, someday you are going to die. Now look around this coffee shop. Every 'fecker' in this place is going to die someday too. And *I am* going to die someday too, and I'm the biggest 'fecker' there is." Silence, a startled expression and then laughter. Like pennies from heaven, laughter.

When we arrived home, in keeping with the lightened mood, Deidre reminded me of her research on finding a puppy – as if I could forget – and treated me to the news that we would be going to see it tomorrow afternoon. The things we do for love.

The next morning saw the momentum continue, with Deidre leaving early to have her nails done by *another* beautician and when I collected her, she said that she had informed the beautician about the diagnosis and was relieved to have told another confidant, and I noted that she had been able to relate the story herself.

That afternoon we drove to Banbridge, south-west of Belfast and approximately ninety miles from home, collecting Conan and Suzanne on the way, to choose our new puppy. There were nine tiny animals in a relatively small room, but despite that, I could still breathe. Maybe this would work out. I even became involved, suggesting we go for the little female with the tan spot on her nose, and I was quietly delighted the others agreed. So she was to be our pup in a few weeks' time. I paid the deposit and we left, as hunger was kicking in and we had completed our business.

We had a very enjoyable late lunch in a pub in Hillsborough which boasted a welcoming atmosphere, and after the good food, we settled in with a drink of something to chat about the new member of the family – I was warming to this – and we forgot about everything else except the day's events. That is, until Deidre met an old work friend and felt the need to tell her, as she expected the news to come out from her workplace now that she had told her boss and colleagues.

The lady in question was clearly very fond of Deidre and was visibly shaken by the news. After she departed, with promises to keep in touch, we retained the positive mood as we left off Conan and Suzanne and took our time driving home. We talked about the puppy, why I had chosen that particular one – it had a helpless look in its eyes which always brought out the protector in me – what we would call her – no decision yet but nothing to do with Spurs was the clear instruction – and how she would have to become used to travelling in the car. Already this little ball of fluff was attending to her distraction duties, and she hadn't even arrived. We retired early from what had been a successful day in every way, exhausted but content.

Sunday, 2 February, started peacefully, and I accompanied Deidre to mass before going to see my mum in Belfast to take her for lunch. Although I was from the 'Other Side', I had promised myself that Deidre would not lose out in matters of faith or ritual because of that. And the service didn't last that long anyway. Lunch passed as lunch passes, and it was lovely to see Mum in good spirits, not yet knowing what had happened, as we had decided to wait until we were sure of the details of the diagnosis before extending the circle of those in whom we would confide.

That evening we went for an early tea to the new bistro in the city, and again it was a pleasant distraction. As we relaxed after our light meal while waiting for the bill, saying nothing about the day to come, I looked at Deidre and reflected on the week that had passed. It was only the blink of an eye, but I was mesmerised by her handling of everything. To truly love someone is priceless. To truly love and respect someone is way up there, like heaven. Believe me, because now I know.

Monday, 3 February. Another day on tenterhooks. Following last week's experience, we were more prepared, and we met the breast specialist as planned to be given more details and have more tests carried out. During the conversation, as panic battled with reason to interpret what we were hearing, and when it hit me all over again that it was my lady being discussed, I exhaled heavily and slumped forward slightly in despair. They looked at me as if I had entered the room unexpectedly, and I raised my hand to signal that I was okay. If only.

As she prepared for the tests, I was assigned to the waiting room. Last week all over again. As my mind raced, the questions came thick and fast. *How can this happen* to ordinary decent people, probably most of whom have children, partners and other loved ones? Only a short time ago they were probably planning for the weekend, wondering what to make for dinner or how they would get through to the next payday. The big issues could have been schooling, Brexit or a soap opera's latest twist, but suddenly they are cast into this vicious cycle of pain and fear.

Still affected by the previous week's experience, I was sat facing a man, and as we made eye contact, I decided to speak instead of sitting through this insufferable silence.

"It's not pleasant," was my opening gambit.

"No, it's not." And as his expression softened, I thought it was worth a try.

"Have you been here before?" was only marginally better than "Do you come here often?" but I was trying.

"No. It's the daughter, and there's radiation, so I have to bring her."

"Oh right, my goodness." *Where do I go now? No clues there.* "Have they told you much about it?" Even I didn't know what I meant.

"She would be unable to make the journey herself, as it's nearly two hundrit meal. So I tuck her."

"Jesus, 200 miles?" I could not stop myself.

"Yes, but it's the nearest hospital that does this kind of thing."

"Well, she's very lucky to have a dad like you." It sounded patronising, but I genuinely meant it. Based on my thoughts about last week, he might not have told her he loves her but he had certainly shown it. And much more.

Just then Deidre appeared again, her scans and tests

completed for another day. I wished him luck and we left the building in silence. As we crossed the car park, I felt the need to say something, "We will fight this together and win." Fine words indeed, but they say timing is everything, and immediately I sensed that they were the right words at the wrong time. Before starting the car, Deidre suggested calling with two close friends, Tom and Marie, as she wanted to tell them. They are the type of people you want with you in a crisis, and this was a crisis. They act, speak and listen with authority. They are the type of people who if they agree with a point you are making, you know you must be right.

When we arrived at their front door, they immediately sensed something was very wrong and bypassed the usual frivolities. Marie ushered Deidre away to a quiet room, while Tom directed me to the kitchen, whereupon I related the story in the knowledge that Deidre would be doing similar. Tom, while obviously shocked, contained his reactions and allowed me to say everything I felt the need to. I outlined the story and he remained attentive despite my beginning to ramble, drawing a comparison in my shock to an earlier upsetting experience in my life. Tom gathered that I was struggling and gave me the space to recover my composure and run him through the story again.

When the four of us convened, it was clear that Marie had also been a comfort to Deidre, who appeared more settled, and her remark that Deidre and I were made for each other was exactly what I, if not Deidre, needed to hear. I will cherish that as long as I live. After tea and biscuits, we knew it was time to go, and, promising that we would keep them posted, we left with their good wishes comforting us on our way. That evening, without agreeing to anything, we avoided any mention of Deidre's condition. Enough had been said for one day, and there was another consultation tomorrow. Somehow we slept that night.

Occasionally in life we meet the very person we need to at the exact time we need to, and in Deidre's oncologist, we met that person. As if the breast, lungs and liver were not bad enough, there was the lingering fear about her bones. I did not say it, but even *I* knew that cancer in the bones would make remaining positive even more difficult. This oncologist – an Italian, we discovered – was a very pleasant lady and a ray of sunshine, emanating an upbeat and 'can do' spirit from the moment we met. After recapping on everything we had already been told, she was able to confirm that there was no cancer in Deidre's bones. Oh yes! But she did struggle to describe what the wastage highlighted in the X-ray actually was. When she made what was, I think, her third attempt at a description, I burst into laughter, as I realised that she was trying to explain that it was due to old age – nothing more sinister. I had never been so grateful to hear my lady described as old. At last a victory of sorts. Without wasting any time, our new friend the oncologist outlined the treatment plan Deidre would be undergoing, and we were surprised but pleased, if a little apprehensive, to hear that the first session was scheduled for Thursday coming.

She explained that they had decided to waste no time, as the way forward was clear, a decision with which we wholeheartedly agreed. The wonderful oncologist outlined what would happen: six chemotherapy sessions supplemented by biological treatments with drugs neither of us had heard of but would quickly become acquainted with, and as they would all be administered near home, thus making it convenient, things, give or take a cancer or three, were actually starting to look up.

Deidre listened intently, asking for clarification where necessary, but I understood that she remained anxious to get to the bit she really wanted to hear: how long did she really have? As she was still unaware of my brief encounter with the breast specialist the previous week, she needed something to hold on to, something to enable her to believe that all the pain and discomfort would be worth it – many more years of life.

The oncologist came across very positively while managing not to answer Deidre's big question. Even if she wanted to, she couldn't. No one could. But she did say, "You'll be fine," which was massively uplifting for us both. I suggested that we had gone as far as we could go for this session and reasoned that we were not too bad after all, and certainly better than yesterday. On the way back Deidre bought a couple of new items of clothing, just to take her mind off things. As you do. It seemed to work, and, again, that evening we slept.

4

Stage 4 metastatic breast cancer *de nuvo*, which had spread extensively to the lungs and liver. It's not much when you say it fast, but this was the diagnosis. It meant that there were cancerous growths in Deidre's breast, liver and lungs. Try taking that in for a start. But what did it mean?

You might choose to google the condition to see what it says. We seem to google everything these days. I was afraid to go near the Internet initially, but quickly succumbed. For the record, stage 4 means it is the most advanced stage of cancer and is diagnosed when it has 'metastasised', spread to another part, or parts, of the body. It does this by breaking away from the original tumour and travelling through the bloodstream or lymph system. The term 'metastatic' also describes a cancer which has started in one part of the body and has travelled elsewhere. A doctor will name it by the part of the body where it originated, the primary cancer. For example, breast cancer that spreads to the lung is called metastatic breast cancer, not lung cancer. It is treated as stage 4 breast cancer, not as lung cancer.

It is also called advanced cancer, secondary breast cancer or metastatic breast cancer. It is incurable at this point but may be controlled with treatment for some years. What a remarkable statement. 'Incurable' and 'for some years' in the one sentence. Incurable is the word no one wants to hear.

So Deidre's cancer started in the breast, travelled to the lungs and liver, and we can be grateful it never made it to the bones. There is no cure, only lifelong treatments, combinations of chemo drugs and biological treatments. If a patient is fortunate enough to survive for a number of years, it is likely that the cancer will get wise to the drugs and find a way to nullify their effect and return. At this stage a different set of treatments will have to be administered. If they exist. There is much, much more available to sufferers than in years gone by, and for that we are thankful beyond words. But there is no cure unless something astonishing happens in our lifetime. And so we live in hope.

This must be on Deidre's mind every second of every day. How can it not be? But then we are tantalised with the hope that the treatment can prolong life for years to come. Years? Great, but how many? Two, three, twenty, thirty? No one will say, because no one *can* say. I think of people whose diagnosis is effectively a death sentence, when they are given six months or less and barely make it. Only now can I even begin to imagine the anguish of their final days.

Deidre decided it was now time to tell my mum and

wanted to be with me when the news was delivered. I agreed and we headed off. I phoned on the way to say we intended to call. It was not as if my mum had plans, and she would be delighted to see us, while not knowing our purpose. As we travelled, I wondered if it would ever stop raining.

"Mum, we have something to tell you." Deidre had delegated delivery to me again and it seemed appropriate. "Unfortunately, Deidre has been to the hospital and she has cancer," – my mum clearly did not take it in – "but we are going to fight this and she is going to be okay." *Here I go again.* Then, as if synchronised, they both began to cry, and I, as always when under stress, continued to talk. "The oncologist has been very positive, and they have a treatment plan in place, and it starts tomorrow... It's all going to be okay." There was nothing more to be said, as both Deidre and my mum needed a pause to compose themselves.

My mum looked straight at her. "I'll be praying for you every night, love. You have a treatment plan already? Praise the Lord." I had heard statements like this all my life and for much of it ignored them, but, finally, I got what my mum was saying. As humans, we must have faith. My mum has boundless faith, and she keeps it simple; and simple was just what we needed. As we had done what we had set out to, including tea, coffee and buns, we decided to go.

We all hugged and said our goodbyes. As we drove, I could see Deidre was exhausted, physically and, no doubt, emotionally, so when she started to doze, I stayed silent, kept my eyes on the road and tried to think of happier times.

We were only just back when my phone buzzed. It was a text from my brother. I assumed my mum had told him, and I had no problem with that, although on balance, I would have preferred to have spoken to him myself. I read his text, and, naturally, he expressed sympathy and best wishes and offered to help in any way he could. He ended by saying that he understood. It was then it came back to me that my brother had been diagnosed with bowel cancer nearly ten years earlier.

Deidre and I had visited New York in early December that year and, as planned, by me at least, had become engaged. When I hosted the 'boys', my work colleagues, Christmas night, I planned to announce my good news early in the evening, before the festive spirits took over. My brother, although he did not work with us, was an associate member of the gang and had been invited. I collected him from the train station in good time so that he could help me with the preparations, and it would allow me to tell him first. He was genuinely happy, and we hatched a plan for how we would maximise the dramatic effect of my announcement.

When the guys arrived and the noise levels began to rise, but just before I was about to give him the nod to bang a tumbler with a spoon, he said that after having seen the doctor earlier in the week, he was going for tests on the Monday coming. I remember looking at him, and he explained that he had been going to the loo a lot and Mum had made him go to the surgery.

"Piss or crap?" I asked, unable to conjure up a more acceptable way of enquiring.

"Number twos," he responded more politely.

"Okay, well, keep me posted." And that was that, until the end of the following week, by which time he had received his diagnosis and the bottom dropped out of our worlds.

My little brother was a sturdy type, rarely ill, and he had no bad habits to speak of, so how could this happen? The family was worried sick, and I could see the effect it had, naturally, on my parents. We rallied around him, led admirably by his wife, and his operation and rehabilitation were successful to the extent that over the subsequent years, because there were no obvious signs of his cancer, I assumed he was better, and if he had not occasionally mentioned it, I would have forgotten. But for the first time, it really did dawn on me that he was not, nor would he ever be, cured. Now I was closer to understanding. And, also, I realised that if anyone could genuinely grasp what Deidre could be going through, it was my brother.

*

It had become clear that Joanne, her long-time friend and colleague and, more recently, style advisor, had also been quick off the mark in suggesting that Deidre should join a series of Instagram and WhatsApp self-help groups for women suffering from cancer and who wish to retain a sense of fun and glamour in their lives. These media provided her with the opportunity to hear current, true-life testimonies from people who were in similar or worse positions than herself, and almost immediately they helped her to gain a more positive perspective. She was learning, and the learning was good. My gratitude, as a partner, to all you wonderful people. You will probably never get to know how inspirational you have been.

The Internet is probably the greatest advance in human communication since language itself, providing information, entertainment and analysis, and bringing old and new friends together. It can also be a curse. Inevitably, Deidre began to google this, that and the other thing related to cancer: the different forms, treatments, side effects, and of course, life expectancy. I tried to keep up, hoping to quell the flames of concern but very quickly realised resistance was futile. There is bad news out there, and you don't have to look too hard to find it. Her holy grail was, naturally, "How long am I going to live?" even though she knew there could be no definitive answer.

Her search also took more traditional lines, and before long an avalanche of books arrived. I began reading them, carefully identifying those which looked likely to provide constructive messages and designating those which appeared more downbeat, and there were many, to the bottom of my sizeable book closet. The variety was impressive, ranging from lifestyle-enhancing and positive-thinking guides to beating cancer, written by PhDs with impossibly taut features and perfect teeth, to academic research which tended to pour cold water on the aspirational, motivational genre by producing statistics to prove that one's mood, up or down, has no effect on the cancer at all. The latter category immediately found their way to the book closet.

There were the personal testimonies, one of which I think was called *F*** You Cancer*, a call to arms of which I was fully supportive, and the author not only wrote the book but made videos, and by God she could dance. Deidre took comfort from them, particularly in these early stages, although she was adamant that she would not be producing books, videos or podcasts. For me, following my drunken performance of *Riverdance* in only a pair of light blue Calvin Kleins to an audience of one, my dancing career had already been consigned to the dustbin of history.

Each evening our reading choices were no longer a whodunnit or a dark psychological thriller, but a new angle on the only subject in town. In most the author related their journey through diagnosis, treatment and, hopefully, recovery, as we all love a happy ending. I homed in on one book, a rather dry, academically based and overly expensive text, and when its opening chapters sought to prove through statistic after statistic that there was absolutely no correlation between how we think and recovery from cancer, I abandoned it after only five chapters. Aside from its content, it had committed the cardinal sin: it was boring. I was worried that Deidre would become overwhelmed by the information but could do nothing about it, so I did the sensible thing by trusting her and, where possible, discussing the latest disclosures and offering a perspective. Neither of us wanted to go under at this early stage, so we reaffirmed to enjoy each day as the blessing it truly was. Difficult, but worth trying.

*

How does anyone receive a diagnosis like this and stay sane? We acknowledged that there were many people in worse positions than ourselves, both in terms of their diagnosis and their means to deal with it. We were comfortably off, lived in a lovely house with two nice cars and had pensions to look forward to. My heart truly goes out to people who face a greater struggle to get through, and I hope every one of them makes it to happier days. In an ideal world we would all achieve that. But in this world, when it is you and your own, everything you have becomes a tool in the battle, and all resources and advantages available will be employed in an effort to survive. We knew it was important to keep saying that to ourselves. We would fight it and win, no matter what the odds.

Wednesday, 5 February, was one of those days in which nothing of significance was due to happen, as the events occupying us had either taken place the previous day or were about to happen on the next one, or in this case both. It gave us time to reflect on how much we had been through and what was to come in the days ahead. If we had been able to plug in and recharge our batteries, we would have.

Thursday, 6 February, was, however, a big day. I thought I had experienced many big days in my life. Exam results, job success, sexual awakening, sporting or musical events, even being in London for a big-screen viewing at their new stadium of Spurs' Champions League Final (defeat). I cannot say, "The day my child was born!" nor, in all honesty with the benefit of hindsight, would the day I got married come to mind. No, this was the biggest day, and this was what it is all about: being there for the ones you love.

This was the first day of Deidre's biological treatments, the first two of which would be administered on a different day from the chemotherapy treatment in an effort to spot any dangerous side effects, and if so, their source. Not much at stake then. Deidre was relieved to be getting started, and I was pleased that she was pleased. As the drugs, the 'biologicals' as they became known, were to be delivered intravenously, she was not so apprehensive, as this was not the worst way for them to enter her body. As we sat in the waiting area, albeit in a different block of the hospital than previously, I was again struck by all that had happened in such a short time. But here we were, and Deidre was doing well, awfully well. The wait was like teeing off at the first golf hole with people watching – you just wanted it to be over. We inadvertently made eye contact, so I smiled and she smiled back. Of course she would, but she did appear relaxed. She was ready for this, and although I dearly wanted to hug her, I did not want to become emotional, so I reverted to counting the tiles on the floor.

It was time, and Deidre set herself up on the bed as directed by the nurse, who was very warm and friendly but also businesslike. The drug packs were encased in heavy plastic and reminded me of those given to my dad a few years earlier, except that those contained blood. Apart from slight irritation at the point of entry, the treatment passed without incident, as if she had been doing this for years. Once the injection process had been completed and the drugs were flowing into her body, we sat. And we sat. And we sat.

Several hours passed, reading a book, scanning the newspaper and smartphone, and occasionally, we chatted. I then called my boss to keep her in the picture, as my work colleagues were very supportive, and like my friends, they probably did not realise how helpful they were. She was as understanding as always, and in a way the conversation brought home to me the reality of our situation. It was not simply a bad dream from which I would awake. For me, however, being here in the hospital was oddly therapeutic, and while Deidre did experience a mildly irritating sensation – not me on this occasion – she did not feel any pain. I think we were both comforted by the knowledge that we were doing something. We were fighting back.

As Deidre was fully coherent, she was able to text friends and work colleagues, catch up on the latest news and gossip, read articles — probably on cancer – many of the things she did not have time to do when she was working so hard. I had been in hospital twice before, with pneumonia, or three times if you count being born, and while neither could be listed as one of my preferred destinations, this ward felt quite homely. I permitted myself a gentle laugh as I considered the frequency with which we would, hopefully, be here for the rest of our lives.

Having finished one of the longer chapters of my novel by Tony Parsons, I decided to stretch my legs and get a coffee. I signalled my intent to Deidre as if I was lifting a cup to my mouth, and she raised her hand, palm forward, as she always does when she is indicating that she is on an important call. And she is never on an unimportant call. I ambled down through the ward, and while the staff looked busy and hurried, each of them had time to exchange a smile or an acknowledgement of some kind.

As I re-entered our ward, I saw a face I recognised but couldn't place: an elderly, distinguished gentleman. After a brief facial-recognition process in my mind's eye, I remembered. He was the owner of my favourite Italian restaurant in the city, or anywhere for that matter. Family owned and authentic, with great food and quirky service, he was always able to select the most suitable bottle of wine, or two, for our chosen dish. It was strange seeing him out of his natural environment, although I readily acknowledge he was entitled to his own life outside the restaurant. But then, of course, I realised. He was also here with a loved one, and when I stole a further glance, that someone was obviously his wife. I did not attract his attention, as I did not want to intrude on a private moment, but I couldn't help observing them for a little longer, as his attentiveness to her touched me. This was devotion. *Good luck, sir, to you and your wife.* I looked at Deidre, who had completed her call and was scanning the ward, and felt nothing but warmth and, yes, devotion.

The nurses called in every so often to check that all was going well. They were clearly very busy but managed to spend long enough to show they cared, and believe me, their care was matched by our gratitude. They are angels who walk the earth. The whole process took eight hours, but it did not drag. Once the nurse confirmed that Deidre was good to go, we packed up and said our goodbyes. It had all passed extremely well, but the next challenge, which would come immediately, was to test how she would react to the drugs.

We spent the rest of the day waiting for something to happen to her. We were well aware of the scare stories about side effects such as hair loss, from head and body, and severe pain, but we knew it was far too early. The forthcoming chemotherapy treatments would be the bruising encounters, but it would be good if the biologicals did not affect her adversely.

Terese, the wig specialist, called early that evening, following the arrangement made in Newry, and she was a breath of fresh air. To make matters even better, it transpired that both she and Deidre are from the same neck of the woods, and Deidre knew of her husband and where she lives. The distraction brought about by the small talk was helpful, and the lady herself had some story to tell, with Deidre hanging on to every word of it.

Deidre was scheduled to see Terese several times in the near future, and I could tell that she was looking forward to it. Wonderful! By now she was receiving heartwarming cards, texts and messages from so many family members, friends and work colleagues, and the house quickly resembled the Chelsea Flower Show. I can testify as to how uplifting they were. You hear about people saying how thankful they were to receive people's good wishes and prayers, but observing her, I could see that they were genuinely helpful.

She must also have been gaining in strength, as she took the time to express gratitude to all the well-wishers and even thanked me for the "immense" support I was giving her. While I did not need it, I appreciated it. She even acknowledged that in the past, before her diagnosis, she could become a little irritated by my frequent positivism, but she now appreciated its value. I dared to think that, ever so slightly, our efforts were showing some benefits, even if only two weeks into our unchartered journey.

Every day had been a challenge to be met, a hurdle to be jumped, a mission to be accomplished, an objective to be achieved, but as the initial shock of the diagnosis was beginning to ease, I detected a faint ray of light at the end of a very long, narrow tunnel. Faint but detectable. We can spend years with someone, share our innermost feelings, hopes and concerns, but can we ever possibly know everything that person, no matter how close, is thinking and fully appreciate what they are going through? What was Deidre really contemplating? What was in that place where only she could go? She had referred to her concerns about her life expectancy, but we had only skimmed the surface, as we were not yet ready. For now, every distraction was a good one, taking our minds somewhere else – where possible, somewhere good. But in her most private of moments, her loneliest place, was she as frightened as I imagine we all would be? That was the thought which tormented me: that she was suffering and lonely in a way she could not share.

*

Friday, 7 February, took us into our third week. Deidre had chemo treatment in the morning and with the initial infusion felt an immediate pain where the breast tumour was. She said after that was delighted that she was now fighting back after the chemo. In fact, everything had gone so well that we decided to have lunch in the new bistro at a local hotel, and I was delighted that she was regaining her appetite. We had been forewarned that her sense of taste and hunger would be among the first casualties of the chemo side effects, and we were not naive enough to believe she would escape completely, but for now, no pain was definitely gain.

On the way home I noticed a sale in her favourite shoe shop, and after a quick detour at the next the roundabout, she purchased three pairs of trendy trainers which would easily enhance her new, non-workplace wardrobe. I will never again doubt the therapeutic effect of clothes and shopping. She tried them on with enthusiasm, describing the various outfits they would go with, and I could have kissed those trainers. First chemo completed, and week three commenced with a welcome, peaceful evening and some sleep.

*

You are very average; smile and get on with it. I am a great believer in affirmations, positive statements of intent formulated to present the desired state as if it is current reality. Or something like that. I had been playing about with them for years, with varying degrees of success. The skill is to keep it real and remain focused on the goal. The goal, however, must be within your potential to achieve. Therefore, *I enjoy running 5k twice per week* is a reasonable affirmation, unless there is some reason why this could never be achieved – no legs perhaps. *I will win the lottery* is less so because it relies on luck rather than potential, provided a ticket has been bought in the first place. In pure affirmation terms, therefore, it is much less likely to be achieved than the 5k run, despite being infinitely more desirable.

I had been tentatively introducing affirmation statements to Deidre but was being careful not to overdo it and put her off, as that is always possible. So, over the past few days and to keep me focused, I had been thinking of a suitable new affirmation for myself. I toiled, trying to be original, aspirational and authentic until, in my current situation, with everything going on in my head, the appropriate affirmation came into my head (see above). Sometimes reality bites and it just won't let go. I smiled, acknowledged my averageness and decided to get on with it.

To my delight, when I raised the idea of her writing affirmations, Deidre confided that she had already created a few and was reciting them every day, along with prayer. They are not mutually exclusive, despite the protestations of some, either on the religious or secular side of the fence. I do not know anyone who would sensibly argue against doing one's best and seeking to achieve their potential; and whether that be through prayer and/or affirmations, or neither, each to their own. We talked for an hour or so and became engrossed in affirmation statements and how to structure them for best results without ever disclosing our own to each other. They may or may not work for us in the future – and I believe they will – but they provided one of the most relaxing hours we had spent since early January, and for that alone I was grateful. The rest of Saturday passed without incident.

When we rose the next morning, Deidre had clearly suffered poor sleep due to chest pain, a horrible side effect. Thankfully, it eased as the day progressed, and although it had taken a lot out of her, she remained stoic, reasoning that if this was the price of chemo, it was a price worth paying. It was distressing to watch her, but I said nothing except to confirm that as it was Sunday – we knew where I would be going.

My mum had worked as a doctor's receptionist for over fifty years and had retired at eighty-three only because my dad had taken ill and she did not want to leave him for longer than necessary. She keeps it simple in her faith and lifestyle and has never looked for hidden meanings in anything. All matters of religious belief are taken at face value, and she will be able to produce one example of anything she wants to prove, usually related to God's lifesaving interventions, despite an avalanche of evidence to the contrary. Unfortunately, as I had not divulged the full story of Deidre's condition, her examples only served to mildly irritate me, but when I snap at her ever so slightly, I immediately feel remorseful and try to make up for my transgression by encouraging her to educate me with further examples. I think some people call it 'suffering in silence'. Of course, it was never that bad, and quite simply a family trait that when we complain it actually means we are enjoying ourselves.

Thankfully, Conan and Suzanne had come up for the evening, and as a treat we went to the local swanky hotel bistro for a meal and couple of drinks. Their enthusiasm for life and each other is infectious and was great medicine for Deidre. She had raised two wonderful young men, and I hoped that she would enjoy them for many years to come. These occasions, even so early in the journey, were greatly appreciated, and I was beginning to detect a correlation between Deidre having a warm family evening and her sleeping that night. And she did, until Monday mid-morning.

5

As a child I was terrified of the Devil. He was some boy, the Devil. I say 'he' because we were taught that he was a 'he', and when we were young, only boys were bad. He was everywhere, trying to make you do wrong things and, it appeared, succeeding regularly. He was always seeking idle hands, and being of a somewhat lazy disposition, I considered myself to be under particular threat. He was obviously responsible for my pangs of jealousy and spite when I didn't get my own way, and I am sure it was his fault I messed my pants when out playing by the river one day when I was at primary school. From fearing the Devil, I progressed to fearing those who talked too much about Satan, as he was also known, as they seemed to do it with relish. Fear of Satan became something of a weapon in regulating our behaviour, because if we were bad, as in not washing behind our ears, picking our noses or looking at the women's underwear section in the catalogues my mum received every Christmas, we would go to hell, with its eternal flames, to see the Devil.

Then, as we became older, there were the other obvious agents of Satan: the headmaster at school, with his cane; bullies; rival gangs; the girlfriend's father; the mother-in-law; failure; illness; and fear of death. The most serious of illnesses went by a name we all feared: cancer. People would choose not to use its name, so traumatic was even the mention of it to mere mortals. There will be very few who have not suffered a loss of some kind due to this most destructive of conditions. I remember, when we were small boys, a friend's mother died from cancer. We didn't understand what was happening, but to see how she changed – losing weight, her hair and even her voice, and watching my friend crying helplessly – was an experience I have not forgotten.

Three of my grandparents – I was too young to really get to know my dad's mother – were taken by this devil, but now it was breathing down my neck. It had chosen to attack my life partner, and it was difficult not to take it personally. In whatever way we feel and describe evil, be it within a religious or secular context, cancer, for me, is evil, as it attacks people in any part of the body in the most painful, soul-destroying and humiliating ways. Indeed, the Cancer Institute uses the image of the killing of the serpent (as in the Garden of Eden) as its emblem. Well, if it's a fight you want, Mr Devil, cancer, we are up for it.

Deidre saw the oncologist again, who confirmed there were no issues with the ECG, and we were elated. I neglected to inform Deidre of my decision, on our behalf, to take on Mr Devil, as she might not have fancied the odds quite so much, and as if to confirm this, she suffered another bad night due to the return of the chest pains.

The discomfort continued through the morning but thankfully eased, as before, in the afternoon. This was important because Tuesday, 11 February, was when our plan to live it up whenever we could was to take a new, exciting direction as we headed off to the Slieve Donard hotel for a couple of nights. After check-in, Deidre had a couple of treatments, of the relaxing kind this time, while I swam and steamed myself tomato red. All was good. As I was lying, 'relaxing', with the sweat pumping out of me, and reflecting on our situation, I was grateful that we had some money put aside 'for a rainy day', as it does make things easier. This was not going to be the retirement we had planned, but we had worked and saved for most of our lives, and I did not intend to feel guilty about enjoying whatever time Deidre, or I for that matter, had left.

In this spirit, we had booked a very trendy restaurant near the hotel which was open early in the week, unlike many eateries. These were the nights we loved, as we would tidy ourselves up and eat tasty food washed down with a glass or two of nice wine. We did not spend nights in pubs or at the races or bingo, so this was our hobby, and a nice one it was too. I had read that it is important for couples to share some hobbies, so, through eating and drinking, we had taken that advice.

We ordered our food and a drink, and all was well, but after the arrival of the first course, a major problem struck. Deidre was suddenly in pain, and despite protesting that she would be fine, she was unable to eat, and I feared that she would have a panic attack. Her pain became unbearable, and we had to leave. She wanted me to remain and have my meal, but I insisted on being with her. When she was outside getting some air, I paid the full bill, as much out of embarrassment as generosity, and mumbled something about her not feeling well. The waiter nodded sympathetically, probably suspecting there had been a row.

After our short walk back to the hotel, Deidre went straight to bed, and thankfully the pain eased sufficiently for her to fall asleep. This was not the evening I had anticipated, and as I sat near the bed watching her, a vision of our new reality appeared to me. I undressed, lay on the bed and stared at the ceiling for as long as I can remember.

Despite the previous night's anguish, Deidre slept well and her pain stayed away until just after midday. It was beautiful outside, sunny but with snow on the not-too-distant Mourne Mountains. She called the triage at the hospital, who confirmed that the pain was a common side effect and advised her to use ibuprofen, which should quickly limit the discomfort. It did.

The *raison d'etre* for the trip was to hold a surprise birthday dinner for Deidre's mum that evening in the hotel restaurant. It had been arranged with her mum's close friend, who would be bringing her on the pretence that only the two of them would be dining. Then, surprise, surprise, we would be there. When we did all meet at the entrance to the restaurant, it was evident that her delight at the surprise was tempered by concern that she did not want her daughter to be exerting herself unnecessarily organising parties, no matter how small, and especially for her. She was, however, genuinely very taken by the gesture, and a quiet, relaxing evening was had by all. Just what the doctor ordered. As the painkillers must have been working, and precious little wine was consumed, we both got the rest we needed.

While sending flowers has been my forgiveness-seeking strategy over the years, I have never been convinced of their real powers over and above their symbolic value. That was until we returned home to find Deidre had received a truly breathtaking bunch from Conan and Suzanne. Despite the fact that the house already resembled a garden centre, these were a priceless addition, and she was truly grateful. "Say it with flowers," was the mantra, and I am now a believer. Following a pain-free day, as she spent time admiring the various arrangements, the pain returned with a vengeance, and she was uncomfortable for the rest of the evening.

Deidre did not rise until noon, having watched morning television, something I had never witnessed her do before. We had a light breakfast, chatting about everything and nothing as the kettle boiled and the toaster did its work. Then we tackled a more serious subject. After much consideration, we decided to opt out of going to the Carpenters tribute concert at the Millennium Forum because, as her immunity could be low, there would be too much risk of infection from being in such close proximity to so many people.

It was a 'no brainer', and Deidre was fully compensated for the disappointment of not hearing someone impersonating Karen Carpenter by the news that Aidan was coming home from London for a weekend break, the best medicine available. (*They Long To Be) Close To You* came to mind. For me, it would be great to see him. We had pulled closer together, the two boys and me, and I was grateful. I think our respect for each other had grown, all realising that without each of us doing our bit, we would not be successful. And I was motivated by their heartfelt appreciation.

To be the outsider coming into the nest, even when the chicks have already flown, can be difficult, particularly in deciding which role to take on: regulating father figure, understanding uncle, joining-in buddy, or despised eternal stranger in the family home. Now, tragically, we all knew my role was as protector of their mother. And this was a mission I was determined to accomplish. Oh, and St Valentine did visit.

On Sunday, 16 February, Deidre was feeling so good she decided to visit two of her friends, another two inspirational people, which was a positive step. Aidan's visit was an outstanding success and he returned to London on the late flight, having refreshed us with an approach and wisdom only he can bring.

The 'feel good' continued the following day, enabling Deidre to be visited by three other friends. I was delighted that she was able to chat with people other than myself or close family, as they would provide new perspectives and, hopefully, lighten her mood. This day, however, day thirteen, was also significant for another reason. It was the day Deidre noticed that she was losing some of her hair. We had been warned to expect this, but she had been doing so well, and now I was afraid that the upset would set her back, undoing the progress we had made. Deidre always had beautiful hair, *I* knew it, *we all* knew it; it was her pride and joy. Cancer makes us ill and then it kills us, but as part of that process, it also seeks to demean us by destroying the very essence of our existence, be it our mobility, our zest or our appearance.

And yet the human spirit enables us to adapt to the most trying of circumstances and the stripping away of each layer of what makes us ourselves. That is what we were now doing – adapting. And we had witnessed the wonders Terese, the wig specialist, could work.

*

Most of the people we wanted to tell had now received the news – family, friends, work colleagues – and they rallied around, wrapping us in an embrace of warmth and good wishes. My own closest friends, Stephen, Paul and Chris, were clearly shocked but provided me with an outlet and the knowledge that the people who mattered were rooting for us. They set up a WhatsApp group enabling us to share concerns and messages of support at any time. It was greatly appreciated.

Deidre's sister-in-law, and long-time friend, Ann, contributed immensely at this time with a fair measure of straight talking and a large helping of practical help, particularly with Deidre's mum, whom she visited regularly. It took a weight off her shoulders. Words are important.

The right ones at the right time can be comforting and inspirational. But actions are often what really matter, and Ann came through, to Deidre's immense gratitude.

Hopefully, we all have people with whom we can be totally comfortable – do-anything, say-anything, tell-anything people, not necessarily family members, who allow us that freedom to be vulnerable. They provide advice, criticism, help, or are simply there when we need them.

A month had passed. We had had no forewarning and nothing to prepare us. Deidre did not find a lump in her breast while having a shower, and her most recent mammogram had been two years ago and was too early to have picked up anything. This realisation, like a punch in the face followed by a kick to the groin, did not help. She had reflected on the sequence of events a few times, wondering how it would have played out if her check-up had been a few weeks later, the lump had been found in time and the cancer had not spread. She did not do this with any bitterness. She graciously accepted the position we were in and put her trust in the doctors and nurses, and in her determination to win. To say it was a shock would be an understatement beyond description. But shock is a strange thing. When in shock, we may not be thinking straight, but just now, we did not need to be totally rational, to weigh up the odds. They were not in our favour. We needed to focus on what positives there were, live from day to day, be brave and hope. Because there is always hope. The specialist had given it to us that Monday four weeks ago, and we would hold on tight. It was our life raft.

Deidre once told me she was one of only 12% of females who qualified as chartered civil engineers, and on top of that, she had risen to a very senior position as a civil engineer in the Northern Ireland Civil Service when women in senior posts was rare, particularly in the civil engineering profession. As a rallying cry, I challenged her to be one of the small percentage of people to recover from this diagnosis. At this stage I told her about my conversation with the breast specialist in which he had said there was indeed hope, and thankfully she was motivated by it, forgetting to challenge me as to why I hadn't told her in the first place. We hope. Even when we cannot expect, we *hope*. It is a powerful emotional tool when there is something, even minuscule, to hang on to. There is always hope. And we pray.

The enemies are loss of hope, despair, self-pity, anger and "Why me?", but in my personal moments, I determined that for all my own failings, I would use whatever I could – listening, empathising and encouraging – to assist Deidre every minute of every day in the expectation that these skills would probably serve us much better than jumping out of planes without a parachute, driving fast cars or lashing in Martini cocktails, and there was only one bad guy we had to defeat: Big C, but not me in this case, as that is my current nickname.

Her treatments were crucial, and the biggest break we had was for the health professionals to identify the treatment plan immediately and start the sessions right away. There would be a combination of chemo and biological drugs, and they would be administered through a drip. Chemotherapy uses anti-cancer (cytotoxic) drugs to destroy cancer cells. The drugs circulate throughout the body in the bloodstream. Chemotherapy for secondary breast cancer can relieve symptoms. It can also control the cancer and improve quality of life for a time, but as we know, it cannot cure the disease. For some people, treatment can control the cancer for many months or years. We prayed for it to be years.

Also included in her treatment, in addition to chemo, were targeted cancer drugs: the monoclonal antibody trastuzumab (Herceptin) and pertuzumab (Perjeta). Herceptin targets and blocks a protein that stimulates breast cancer cells to grow and multiply. It only works if your breast cancer cells make too much of a protein called HER2, another term we would quickly become familiar with. HER2 is a protein that helps breast cancer cells grow quickly. Breast cancer cells with higher-than-normal levels of HER2 are called HER2-positive. These cancers tend to grow and spread faster than breast cancers that are HER2-negative but are much more likely to respond to treatment with drugs that target the HER2 protein. All invasive breast cancers are likely to be tested for HER2 either on the biopsy sample or when the tumour is removed with surgery. Many of us are informed about the drugs we or a loved one may be about to receive, and we are warned of the possible side effects. But how much do we actually take in? As I have been receiving drugs for asthma for years, I will take what I can get whenever I can get it, and thankfully I am still here. We are grateful for the drugs and whatever is in them.

*

Friday, 21 February, was something of a landmark in that it was to be the first time we were to separate since the news. Kathy, Deidre's friend and possibly closest confidante, would be coming up to stay. This was a breakthrough and would be the best kind of therapy. Their domestic responsibilities meant that they could only meet every so often, but they thrived on each other's company, often chatting into the early hours.

I was to visit my mate Stephen, and I also was looking forward to the change of scenario and company, and our egos could withstand knowing that we were looking forward to being with someone else for the evening. I made it to Stephen's house, and as we thirstily downed some beers, we agreed not to make use of our recording studio on this occasion, as we would have ample opportunities over the forthcoming weeks. Instead we took stock of our different worlds. As I recounted our story to him, with any updates since we last spoke, I could not help but reflect on his own experiences over recent years with his daughter. As I asked him about Lauren and he returned the compliment of updating me, while marvelling at her remarkable progress, I realised that with the greatest will in the world, until now I had not the faintest idea as to what he, his daughter and his family had been going through.

I can still remember the morning he called me at work to say he would be late as he and his ex-wife were calling to Lauren's school as she did not want to go in, citing constant headaches, and they were concerned that she was being bullied and making excuses. However, bullying was not the reason; tumours were. Several years of major operations, and endless consultations later, their beautiful young lady was living a life as close to normal as she could. The 'new normal' we laughingly called it, referring also to my own circumstances. During this conversation, not only was I grateful for the opportunity to talk, but I developed a deeper appreciation for my friend, confidante and fellow band member.

Needless to say, I ended up quite drunk, and I am reliably informed that I enjoyed dinner. He is ten years younger than I am, with hollow legs, and he's also very understanding. Next morning we had breakfast, and when I left, I think we both knew we had been good for each other.

More importantly, Deidre also had a great night with her friend, and I was sure that she would have got a lot off her chest. I am not so self-consumed that I need to be the only person she could or should confide in. The more they meet, the merrier, as far as I am concerned. Thank you, Kathy.

Following our respective late nights, Saturday went peacefully, with Kathy and I passing as ships in the night. Deidre and I exchanged stories over coffee – lots – of how our evenings went, except that, I confess, I neglected to mention that I could barely remember dinner. Anyway, I was entitled to cut loose just this once. Because of, or despite, our previous night's experience, we slept soundly, and the world, for this moment, was a better place.

Refreshed and ready for action on Sunday morning, we decided to drive to Belfast to visit the house Conan and Suzanne were interested in buying, and, to their relief and mine, it received the 'Mum seal of approval'. As we had come this far, we continued our journey down to Deidre's mum for her regular visit, having dinner in a very pleasant local restaurant, and the following day, on the way home, we called on her brother, Peter, and sister-in-law, Ann.

We were back in time to attend a restorative yoga class with our teacher, John, who had also become a friend, and his empathetic approach helped Deidre complete the session. I like the idea of having just completed a yoga session rather than the experience of actually doing it. And the teacher and I? We have an understanding. The restorative version of yoga is much less active than the version Deidre had previously practised, but it was a good start. I knew she was quietly pleased with her achievement, and she needed more of this.

Later, two close friends, Sean and Clare, called, and it was relaxing to be able to sit and talk about everything and nothing with them. While the evening's events were not earth-shattering, they were enjoyable. They were normal. And that was what we needed right now.

Normality continued, and the week drifted by

uneventfully in that we woke, did things, ate, slept, woke, did things, ate, slept, and so on. That sense of routine, the one I always claimed to despise, I now embraced wholeheartedly.

On Friday we treated ourselves to dinner in our favourite restaurant, and to make things even better, friends of Deidre's, who had heard her news and were delighted to see her, paid for our meal, not an empty gesture in this establishment. However, it was not the money; it was the expression of friendship we appreciated. To witness the genuine concern and warmth on the faces of those who knew her and met her after her news broke was uplifting and humbling. It was a lovely night and we slept well.

Thankfully, because it had been a quiet night, we were clear-headed for Deidre's bone marrow injection on Saturday morning. The term itself sounds frightening, but she did not look apprehensive at all. The nurse came to the house, and after confirming Deidre's identity – as if anyone would falsely volunteer for this injection – they went to another room. After the treatment she was tired and sore but pleased with her achievement and that another step had been taken, another challenge met, so we took it easy for the rest of the day. I had grown to love taking it easy. She did not talk me through what happened earlier, and I had the sense not to ask.

It is Sunday, 1 March, and I am sitting in the kitchen, second coffee and reading the Sunday papers, looking out at a beautiful March late morning – life can be good. Deidre is in bed suffering side effects of yesterday's bone marrow injection – and not so good. Earlier she had become light-headed at Mass and I'd had to help her out of the building.

As we sat together in the pew, going through the session, which involved sitting down and standing up at regular intervals, I sensed something was wrong, as she was breathing quickly and heavily. And of course I asked the stupid question, "Are you okay?"

"Get me out of here," was the response.

"What do you want me to do?" I asked as if oblivious to the instruction I had just received.

"Get me—" but by then I had Deidre by the elbow, lifting and shuffling to the right, as the pew in that direction was clear. As we got to the end of it, and the priest was in full flow, I had Deidre by the arm, and as she was thankfully cooperating, I guided her, in full view of the congregation, down the aisle and out the door. The congregation could not help but see us tottering along the aisle while the sermon was continuing behind our backs. I was both avoiding eye contact and trying to display an expression that what I was doing was indeed a Christian thing, and we were not in any way trying to offend the Lord. But it was unnerving to sense all the eyes on us.

Immediately after we had left the building she began to recover, the fresh air being a welcome tonic. Once home, she didn't feel so bad, but I acknowledged to myself that these occurrences may become more frequent. Now, as she was resting, I looked up from my newspaper and wondered how life can be so wonderful and yet so cruel at the same time. Deidre slept for most of the afternoon and was aching from head to foot when she woke, but as she had no nausea, this would do for now. For tomorrow is a brand-new day.

*

It became a week of cold reality, as Deidre was tired and aching all over and we began to fear that the symptoms would not cease. My feeling of powerlessness returned, but when nothing can be said, it's best to say nothing. Even the most motivational words can be counterproductive if overused or delivered at the wrong time. *When* you choose to say something can be as important as *what* you say.

On Monday afternoon a work colleague called, and he inadvertently was a greater comfort to Deidre than he could have imagined, regaling her with graphic accounts of work-related business, and they laughed and exchanged comments for a couple of hours at least. Deidre was devoted to her profession and the role she had performed, and I feared that she would be unable to let go, and that the consequent withdrawal symptoms would drag her down further. But so far, so very, very good. Perhaps, and not for the first time, I had underestimated her. When she recounted the highlights of their conversation (nothing to worry the Official Secrets Act, be assured), she had clearly been given a great lift, but thankfully there was no evidence of those withdrawal symptoms. Not yet anyway.

Continuing on this crest of a wave, on Tuesday Deidre went to a counselling session arranged through the Action Cancer service and organised throughout the UK and

Ireland. Having been a counsellor, I was intrigued as to how she would react. I hoped she would benefit from the experience and decide to continue, although I did fear the odds were against it, as she was not predisposed to 'pouring your heart out'.

We are different. A blind man on a galloping horse would see that, but it has rarely caused us a problem because I usually always do what I am told. We do not, however, adhere to the male/female characteristics stereotypes. Deidre is the practical, 'get it done' engineer, while I tend to display the traditionally more feminine, feelings-oriented 'let's think this through and consider how we feel about it' approach. Fortunately, neither of us is restricted to only these facets of our respective personalities, as I have never been known to decline a night's drinking with the lads nor Deidre to spend money on handbags and make-up. Therefore, from day one we agreed that as far as what makes us tick is concerned, there is room for both. And nearly ten years down the line, there still is.

I was delighted when Deidre confirmed that she had found the counselling session useful, acknowledging, however, that in her position, any kind of help is graciously accepted. After discussing how the session went, in process terms rather than what was actually said, I was also relieved when she confirmed that she would go back.

It is easy to be territorial, even possessive, when contemplating your partner going over their innermost with a complete stranger. We can wonder if we have been referred to in a positive or negative light. Or worse, not mentioned at all. Any form of possessiveness can be damaging to a relationship, and we are too old for all of that. I am aware that the purpose of counselling is to help the client, and – it may sound strange – the best helper can therefore be a complete stranger who has no interest in the client's disclosures over and above being of genuine assistance by making sense of it all. Anything that was helping *her* was helping *us*.

If the counselling session was unexpected, we were then both offered massage sessions to help us deal with the stress of what we were going through, and while I was prepared to make light of it to friends, I was quietly grateful that the role of the partner was recognised. It was to be in a few weeks' time, and we had the date in our diaries, as nothing would prevent us from getting to that session. Or so we thought. As it turned out, all of those plans would disappear like a thief in the night, as an intervention of seismic proportions would put an end to them, and the world as we knew it.

By Thursday Deidre was tiring, but she was still happy to see a couple who have been her friends for years, and any reason for coffee and cake is a good one in my book. That evening we went to a local bistro restaurant for a light meal, as neither of us had the energy to cook. Deidre seemed strangely down, and to make matters worse, she broke a tooth. While it was not painful and, thankfully, was not at the front of her mouth, it still happened. Her nails, her hair, her teeth. I could imagine what she was thinking, and her mood had deteriorated from earlier in the week, with the next few days being tiring and awkward for her. The new normality.

It was difficult to predict which days would be good for her and which would be bad, and come up with any reason for why they should be one or the other. We talked it over and agreed that we would have to go with the flow, good days, bad days, and be grateful for each, reasoning that many people were in worse situations. Not a particularly benign thought, but we all do it.

This day had been coming, so I couldn't say I hadn't been warned. Deidre had been drawing my attention to some of her hair coming out, but fortunately, while it was obviously thinner, she was by no means bald. But to her she was. Her hair had always been her crowning glory, whether long and curly, or shorter and bobbed, the way I had known her.

She was not as distressed as I feared she might be, but we hadn't left the house yet. Terese had been brilliant in dealing with her, and organising the quite amazing wigs. But now was the day for fitting. There was to be no miracle regrowth, no going back.

I had never thought much about wigs. We had all worn them as fun at some time, and they were too warm for my comfort. I was too young to realise most film stars from the golden age wore wigs, or toupees as they were referred to. What I could never get my head around was why some men chose to wear a red/brown colour of wig when the hair at the sides of their heads was clearly grey for all to see. Talk about realistic; all they needed was a chin strap. It was a matter for themselves, and one which I did not care about. But I cared about Deidre. The wigs made for her looked lifelike, and as we had established, they were, of course, made of real hair.

For many people, wigs perform a valuable service, covering scars and other marks which destroy the confidence of the individual and their ability to enjoy their lives. There is probably a difference between misplaced vanity and necessity, but each to their own. If they enable people to retain their dignity, whatever the motivation, they are good enough for me.

I went with her, although I was unsure as to how much support I would be able to give. The two ladies, Terese and her assistant, had done this before many times and were true professionals, constantly talking and engaging Deidre, and not allowing her to take in what was about to happen for the first time in her life.

I sat there in silence. I had been shaving my head for several years, but this could not have been more different. I genuinely did not know how Deidre would react, and the last thing we needed was another heartbreak.

Terese began the process, and the shaver started buzzing. I held my breath, sitting watching events unfold in the mirror, so I could see the actions and Deidre's reactions as she held my hand and shed a few tears. As the trimmer went to work, one tuff of something flew into the air and descended just as quickly, like autumn leaves from a tree, then another, then another. And another. Terese kept going calmly but firmly, like a mum administering medicine to a child. I was glued to my chair in anticipation of a nightmare, but something else happened. A new face appeared in the mirror, fresh, big eyes, defined cheekbones, and then something truly unexpected, a smile. She looked stunning without the big mop of hair. There before me was the most beautiful woman in the world.

It was as if she had escaped from something. I was not sure what it could have been, perhaps a fear that without her hair she would not look right or was not her true self. But she did look great. Spontaneously, the three of us applauded, and the assistant, who had cried throughout the whole process, unprompted, removed her own wig, showing her head and how realistic the wig had been.

Deidre's wig was applied, and of course it looked realistic, but I had a bet with myself that before long she would be going *au naturelle*. If I had known how great she would look, I would have tried to convince her that a wig was totally unnecessary. But one step at a time. As she placed the mop on her head, the transition was complete, and it was seamless. Deidre came in looking beautiful, and she would be leaving looking beautiful.

I had seen enough to know that she would suit a new, short hairstyle, but that would come. Getting through this was one hell of a hurdle, but she had just managed one hell of a jump.

For now, let's go home.

Several weeks passed, and despite not seeing as many people as previously, those she came into contact with who had no idea about her condition would have gathered nothing from her appearance and demeanour, or they were experts at managing their reactions, and when, playfully, she confessed to a couple of friends, they were genuinely speechless.

Then the day came. There was a loud knock at the door, followed by another, and another. I was indisposed, so Deidre, forgetting everything, went to the door to resolve the issue. Only on this occasion she did so without her wig. Sensing that she had been in a hurry, I made it to the door only to see her, minus wig, smiling at me. I stated the obvious as a question. "You know you don't have your wig on? Are you okay?" She gave a barely audible laugh, opened her hands and shrugged her shoulders. The wig was never seen again, such was her progress. And by the way, the new look was class.

*

As we were settling into our decision to live for the now, with impromptu visits to hotels for a late-afternoon drink or to restaurants for an 'early bird' meal, I decided that it would be a good time to investigate the possibility of buying a new car. New, as in new to me. After browsing online and wandering past car showrooms, usually after they had closed, I became increasingly drawn to the dream car, and once we become drawn to the dream, we begin to articulate why the dream, in fact, makes perfect sense. We agreed that a sports utility vehicle, SUV to those in the know, and what we used to refer to as a jeep, would be good for us, bringing comfort and safety, and more convenient access. All very sensible and laudable. But then...

A Porsche Cayenne. True, it's not a 911 Carrera or

Boxster, but it is a Porsche. And let's face it, that is what matters when you first set foot in this dream world. As a young boy at primary school I took it for granted that I would be rich, famous and drive cars like Porsches or Aston Martins. I had never quite worked out how I would achieve this fame and fortune – actor, singer, guitarist, secret agent, or whatever – as I never quite developed the plan for how this would happen. I just knew it would; that was my destiny in life.

Through the years, however, disappointment, failure and betrayal put a severe dent in these fantasies, and in order to come to terms with the darker periods in life and protect myself, I occupied an alternative reality called, *Someday I will do this. Someday I will have that.* All retained within the dream box but rarely, if ever, opened. And then came the Porsche.

You can convince yourself of anything; I have convinced myself of that. And I was in overdrive. I now had some money, more or less, I had the circumstances in that the long, expensive work-related journeys would be rarer, and slowly but surely I was gaining the motivation. Having seen the car, Deidre was won over, and that was really all that mattered. In all honesty, while the car was for me, it would be for her, and for the time we had left. I am no negotiator, so following Deidre's intervention on my behalf, saving a few hundred pounds, I agreed the sale that day and went about getting the finances together to ensure collection the following week.

Over the next two days a few old friends called to see Deidre. Visits like these continued to give her a reason to pep up, and changes in the conversation with different voices and stories were good for her. For me, it was a chance to reflect, probably when I least needed to. Why, when I had just taken the opportunity to buy my dream car, did I feel so flat? Flat and guilty.

"What's wrong? Are you okay?" I enquired, not for the first time, knowing it can easily become irritating.

"Nothing, really. I'm okay," Deidre responded. But I knew her too well. I decided to have one more go, trying to get the balance right between encouraging her to talk and being a pain in the neck.

"I can't stop thinking about it."

"It?" I responded, feigning ignorance as to what 'it' was.

"Thursday," she offered, but if it were a quiz, I would be deducted a point for needing another clue.

"Oh yes, I know, but I just didn't want to mention it to you." I didn't mention it because I had not remembered, "Are you worried?"

"How could I not be? Who wouldn't be worried about scan results, especially for something like this?" There was neither sarcasm nor impatience in her voice, but I would have deserved it if there had been.

"I can never say I understand fully. More than most, maybe, but not fully." And rather than stop there, off I went, "I do genuinely believe it will be okay, that it will show recession and that the treatments are working."

Apart from her remarkable appearance, I had nothing to base this on, but I felt duty-bound to counter any negative remark with a positive riposte, even when it was not helpful. Like now.

"I know it's irrational, because it has all been going well, but I just can't help worrying."

"Like an exam you have studied furiously for but are still afraid you might fail?"

"Yes, something like that, but…"

"But the stakes are much higher in this instance. Of course they are." And that is the problem with comparisons and analogies; rather than clarifying, they can come across as insensitive and hurtful. I realised Deidre was now tired and needed to stop talking about it, but I was trying to end on a positive note. "The doctors and nurses are wonderful, and they have been very positive, haven't they?" I continued, as I wasn't waiting for a response. "And they will do everything they can, and if anything was wrong, they would have let you know immediately," I rambled. I wasn't sure if this was in fact true, but it sounded good.

"I know all that but… but I'm just frightened, I suppose."

"Naturally. You're only human after all. And I understand."

To be frightened? Yes, that I understood fully as I gave this woman one of the warmest hugs I could manage. But it's the helplessness. The helplessness.

6

Friday, 6 March, heralded a very exciting seven-day period to come, and thankfully also a noticeable upturn in Deidre's energy levels, her best to date, and she wanted to be active. In recognition of this, we took a drive to the village of Moville in Donegal, where we had an invigorating walk along the sea path at the edge of the Atlantic Ocean and part of the 1,600-mile coastline known as 'The Wild Atlantic Way' – a tourist attraction if ever there was one, but to us, simply a place of great beauty – and followed with lunch before a leisurely return journey. That night we slept soundly.

The next few days passed uneventfully, and on Monday Deidre met another work colleague, who, like his predecessor, provided her with updates on the toing and froing, which she, again, enjoyed. She had been blessed with a supportive group of workmates, and they had been blessed with her. Wow! In the evening we attended our yoga class, and if she had worried about struggling, she only had to look at me puffing and blowing for assurance.

On Tuesday we paid a visit to Castle Leslie, a beautiful hotel in County Monaghan we had been to once before, where we walked, relaxed and enjoyed dinner and some wine. To be honest, alcohol consumption was an integral part of our lives, and while Deidre tended to drink small amounts quite regularly, I tended to drink larger amounts even more regularly. To know that she could have a glass or two of wine with dinner was important because it suggested normality and I did not feel the need to imbibe on my own. To our surprise and delight, as we were about to settle the bill, we were informed that it had already been paid by her brother and sister-in-law. A lovely gesture. We visited Deidre's mum on the return journey, and she was grateful for how well things seemed to be going for us.

And then Thursday, 12 March, was the first of two big days. I had conceded from day one that a dog was coming into our lives, and seeing Deidre's enthusiasm every time she mentioned it, I had surrendered unconditionally. If I could keep breathing after her arrival, it would all be grand. The woman selling the pups effectively interviewed us as to our suitability to be owners, and our first visit left us in no doubt about her concern for the homes they were going to. We interpreted this as a very positive thing. Once we knew the pup was coming, the issue of a name came up. As I had been warned not to suggest anything to do with Spurs – Ossie, Ricky and Harry were out, and Chirpy never crossed my mind – I kept quiet. When it really matters, I can bide my time.

Then one morning it came. "I was thinking about a name for the dog." Silence. I wasn't even breathing. "What do you think about Lily as her name?" I could not believe it. Tottenham Hotspur, the other love of my life, while commonly known as Spurs, have an official nickname, 'the Lilywhites', or 'the Lilies'. But I could not give myself away; not yet.

"How come, honey?" Sounded good in the first exchange.

"My father played for Ballymartin Gaelic football team near his home, and they were known as the Lilywhites."

"Okay, we can go with that, as it clearly is very significant to you." *You don't say! Not at all like myself of course!* I decided to delay my disclosure for a couple of days, but by lunchtime I could not contain myself. "You know the way the dog is going to be called Lily? Yes? Well, that is also the official nickname of Spurs, so we are both happy."

I produced the website on Google as if she was actually interested in having it confirmed. And now the day of the dog had come, nearly two months after the diagnosis.

Can a man love two women at the same time (not including one's mother, and I have no sisters)? Does love at first sight exist? Two questions which, like the chicken and the egg, have puzzled humans since romance began. The answer to both, I can now tell you, is yes! Having parked my car, allowing Deidre to go ahead of me, I entered the home of the family we were to buy Lily from, and there she was, being held aloft by my partner. The two of them together; it was love at first sight, believe me, and they were equal first in my rankings. I was never much for dogs, my chronic allergy asthma notwithstanding, perceiving them as too time-consuming and preventing the 'drop everything and go' attitude to life I claimed to prefer.

However, a dog seemed like the perfect consumer of time in the long days ahead, and seeing Deidre's face just that minute assured me that this was going to be one of the best decisions we had ever made. The two of them together imprinted a picture in my mind I will never forget. I was in love with Deidre, now in love with Lily, and in love with the both of them together. It was perfect, and a minute later it was even better as I held her in my arms and she looked up at me without crying, barking or wetting both of us. She just looked and looked and looked. And I looked and looked and looked. And then her mummy tried to bite my leg. Apparently, she was still being protective, but couldn't she tell her tiny daughter was going to be the best-looked-after little pup in pup land?

I was now keen to make my exit and get her all to ourselves, so we paid the very reasonable cost minus the deposit, collected our goody bag the owner had so thoughtfully prepared for us, made the usual excuse about having a long drive home and got on our way. To our surprise and relief, our little baby took to the car and was not at all problematic on the journey. Welcome, Lily.

*

On Friday, 13 March, Deidre woke and was feeling good, a heartening start to the day. As for me, today I was going to own a Porsche. I was aware of the apparent significance of the date, but that had nothing to do with it. I was feeling apprehensive and a bit flat. They say context is everything, and for some reason, buying this big, fancy car aroused slight feelings of guilt. What was I, a non-achiever with a very ill partner, doing thinking he could gallivant around in a big fancy Porsche? But I had committed, and I have to say, so had Deidre. In fact, she appeared to be managing her own guilt complex extremely well.

As we drove to pick up my new vehicle, I thought of the car that was soon to be my ex-vehicle, the car which I'd bought shortly after my father's passing, using some of the money he had left me. Maybe that was it. I felt guilty about dispensing with something which he helped me buy. I was also quite sure that he would not have been impressed by my new acquisition, as he never had any time for 'Fancy Dans', and I think he had me down as a chief suspect over the years. It might have been the fear that they would all discover that I was out of my depth and would laugh at even the idea of me thinking I could buy this car. I am, however, cautious when making a big decision and like to do it in my own time. And this, it appeared, was my own time.

So I was driving with my new puppy and partner, kitted out in shades and expensive casual clothes, all in black, to match the car. I continued to wonder what I was doing all the way into the garage forecourt, when I was met by our beaming sales executive, Mike, a genuinely nice guy. We touched elbows as an alternative to shaking hands, a new fad related to the virus thing everyone was talking about. During an early conversation with him

I mentioned Deidre's condition – it seemed to be the thing to do – and we were totally taken by surprise when he produced a bunch of flowers to rival those currently taking residence in the house. A classy touch, so nothing could go wrong now. We worked our way through all the usual pleasantries, and I even managed to crack a joke and look like I knew what I was doing. That was until we came to the part where I was to actually pay for the vehicle.

As the endless form-filling neared completion, I produced my card in preparation for the big deal to go down. Despite using them regularly, I am apprehensive about non-money transactions until the other guy says something like, "That's okay, sir." Then I relax. I have long lost the feeling that I am not actually paying, but where technology and I are concerned, when there *can* be a problem, there *will* be a problem. I looked at the tiny blue bank card, and I marvelled at how this little blue piece of plastic can be used so easily to move thousands of pounds from one location to another in an instant. I brushed my fingers, admiringly, along the top of the card. Admiringly, that was, until even with my lack of knowledge, I noticed something was not right. The card's surface was not smooth, as it should be, and then my panic button was pressed. The SIM part of the card, the only part that really matters, had fallen off. In fact, I remembered picking up something like that from the bedroom floor a few days earlier and wondering what it was. I knew also that it was now at or near the bottom of the bin at home. I jolted forward, my throat went dry and my anticipated humiliation was underway.

That's what happens when you get ideas above your station, Fancy Dan, a voice from somewhere whispered in my ear. In a matter of seconds, I was about to be exposed as a fraud, and as I could not think of a lie, I chose honesty as the best policy and drew it to the attention of Mike, who took the card from me, looked at it, nodded as if to confirm that indeed the SIM had gone and then looked back at me.

All of a sudden, this guy looked very young, young enough for homework.

"This is very embarrassing," I offered in an effort to take the initiative and press the onus for finding a solution onto my very young sales-executive friend.

"Shall we try the card anyway?" he suggested, thus making me feel that I was the brains behind this operation.

"Yes, of course, and we can see what happens." Not my best moment in problem-solving. In went the card, we waited, and nothing. The golden rule for halfwits and technology is to keep doing the same thing again while hoping for a different result. What was it Oscar Wilde said? Of course, nothing again.

"Where is your bank?"

"In the town," I confirmed, not knowing what was coming next.

"Do you want to go down and explain what happened and see if you can get a new card?" Seriously? I would have agreed to anything, as I was by now looking for a way out.

"Okay, I'll give that a try and then I will get back to you."

You are probably wondering where Deidre and the

puppy were during this. Thankfully, they witnessed none of it, but I now had to explain myself. They had remained in the car anticipating a very quick turnaround and had expressed no interest in the non-event of a car purchase. As I got into the driver's seat, I was met with "Well?", the question which despite being a question always demonstrates advanced knowledge of what I am about to divulge.

"There's a problem. Do you remember the SIM thing I mentioned the other day?" I pressed ahead, not waiting for confirmation. "It was from my card, and now I can't get the money through, so I'm going to go down to the bank to get a new card," I explained while keeping a straight face.

"You are going to do what?"

"I know it sounds daft, but…"

"Daft? You know how long it takes to get a card. Did you talk this over with Mike? Why don't you—"

Just then there was knocking on my window and Mike had appeared. Could things get any worse? I wound the window down and he maintained the 'nothing's wrong' look we had both been practising earlier. "I just thought, why don't you just phone me and I can take the details from there?"

"Yes, of course," I replied, thankful for the potential escape and wishing we had thought of it before confessing to Deidre. "I'll call you from the car and you can take my details. I'll wait until you get back to your desk."

I received the thumbs up and waited, counting the number of steps I imagined it would take him to complete the journey. I called, and he answered as if he had not been expecting me. The transaction worked and I had bought the car. As I turned to Deidre, she completed her sentence, which was, "You didn't need to call from here. You could both have sat at his desk and done it from there."

Looks probably cannot kill, but they can humiliate. A few more forms were adorned with our signatures, and the reception staff instantly fell in love with Lily, who had been kidnapped for a group photograph for the local journal. I took one last look at the BMW, whispered a breath of thanks to Dad and climbed into the driver's seat of the Porsche.

We made it home without incident, but I was nervous, fearful of any further unexpected embarrassment. We took a few photographs in the driveway before adjourning for a coffee, which provided an opportunity to reflect further on buying my dream car. Maybe dreams are not all they're cracked up to be. But it's an amazing vehicle, and that's a start.

Deidre's diagnosis reshaped our lives, and however long we might have together, we were entitled to live as well as we could, and I, like everyone in my position, would do everything to make my partner's life as wonderful as it could be. Of this I was determined, and of this I was proud. *Honey, do you like my new wheels?*

The anticipation of the boys and Suzanne arriving was an excellent distraction for the morning. Aidan had come home from London to see his brother, and then to see his mother, and they would all be very welcome. We were excited and talked about what their reactions might be to seeing the new car in the driveway and then meeting Lily, in Aidan's case, for the first time. We were not disappointed, as they reacted just as we had hoped. Deidre took them to visit one of the local furniture stores, largely as an excuse to get out in the car, and I was grateful for the time alone, as it helped me collect my thoughts.

That evening, as planned, we went to La Sosta, a very attractive family-owned Italian restaurant in the city, where we had a delicious meal, and as it was something of a celebration of us being together, we washed it down with a glass of champagne, some wine and a nightcap.

The owner, the gentleman I had recently seen at the hospital attending to his wife, and one of the most pleasant people on earth, mentioned that he had received some cancellations due to the virus thing which was on the tip of everyone's tongues. He added that luckily most of his regular customers were turning up because, knowing the restaurant, they felt safe. After that, unperturbed, we simply enjoyed the food and Deidre's obvious pleasure at having her family together with her.

And then home to see Lily. I interpreted Lily's bark as something like, "Where the hell were you until this time?" and I suddenly realised going out would, in future, require an additional set of arrangements. But she forgave us as the treats appeared, and we all had our photos taken with our new little bundle of fluff. Perhaps she was hypo-allergenic after all. It was an excellent night out, Deidre was thrilled, and we agreed to do it again within the next few months.

Sunday was everything a Sunday should be: peaceful, restful, Sunday Times and a cooked breakfast with the promise of Sunday dinner to come. Oh, and as we had guests, a glass or two of wine. Next week I would cut back. After the kids left, I felt a bit flat, like at school when the summer holidays were ending, and probably their presence had enabled us to talk about everything except the obvious. I kept wondering about how Deidre was coping with her innermost thoughts and fears, but as the minutes, hours and days passed, and with our various distractions, we did seem to be getting through. We were functioning and finding things to do without aimlessly wasting our time. Many things, so far, had gone in our favour: she was still mobile and in good spirits; fears about her hair, eyebrows, nails and skin had not yet been realised; we were comfortable enough financially to indulge ourselves to some degree; and, most importantly, we were finding out all over again how truly wonderful people can be. The genuine concern and good wishes extended by many were a recognition of Deidre's qualities as a person, qualities which I hoped would sustain her in her journey. We were only at the beginning, but it seemed like we had successfully completed some kind of a first phase.

They say the best chance of surviving cancer is to catch it early: notice differences, heed the signs, listen to your body. All sound advice, and clearly many people continue to walk the earth as a consequence of being on the ball as described. But what if there are no signs? I have heard a significant number of people state that they had no idea what was going on in their bodies, that they were blissfully unaware, that they were simply not receiving any message to tell them something was terribly wrong. We wracked our brains to try to recall if there had been anything to tell us what was happening to Deidre, and apart from the pain that fateful Sunday morning, we could think of nothing. Probably because there had been nothing. Nothing, at least, that we do not associate with the normal travails of modern life. Sense of pressure and not enough time to get everything done. Constant tiredness. Irritation and dissatisfaction with individual circumstances and life in general. A feeling of life passing us by. Stress. I cannot honestly say that Deidre suffered from any these, possibly tiredness and stress from the competing priorities of a busy home and work life, but nothing out of the ordinary, just the pace of the modern world. Was there anything we'd missed? She had previously visited the doctor for a diagnosis of a rash and then a minuscule growth on her leg, but they were ailments in their own right and not linked to anything more sinister.

We tend to laugh about hypochondriacs, and we all know at least one – detailing every sore head, cough or pain – and they are the only people I know who read the directions leaflet in each packet of tablets, noting the possible side effects, many of which are worse than the condition they are meant to cure. We should, however, be vigilant, in the hope that we can identify a symptom which will lead us towards an early diagnosis. I have been coughing and wheezing since childhood, so if I finally succumb to a respiratory failing, I cannot say I was not forewarned. They will blame the years I smoked, not heavily, but I will know it was simply bad luck to have had such fucked-up lungs since birth and that largely through exercise I have been able to maintain a decent, at times thrilling, life. And that is the point. We do everything we reasonably can to notice changes in our bodies, and minds for that matter, but should remember to focus on how well we are doing right now.

For me, the people who are preoccupied with living forever often tend to be the most miserable in their day-to-day lives. Equally, being told you have Stage 4 cancer does little to lighten the mood. I decided to remember who and what I am, what I have come through, and to continue to make plans with Deidre and be mindful that, as we do not know the future, we must try to put something into, and get something out of, every day. It is worth it.

The rest of the week passed quietly, and as the news coverage of the virus was taking centre stage and looking quite serious, we decided to be safe rather than sorry and curtail our travels for a few weeks at most until it was all sorted out, or so we thought. In the meantime, yoga on YouTube and outdoor walks kept us occupied. One niggle, however, was the speculation over how the health service might be affected if the virus caught on and took a hold. This would be very worrying generally, but our only focus was if it would be detrimental to Deidre's treatment plans. After discussing it briefly, we agreed that there was enough to worry about without idle speculation, and anyway, we had seen things like this before: AIDS, bird flu, and so on.

We determined that nothing would prevent Deidre from getting her treatments on time, and on 19 March she successfully completed her third chemo session. It was followed, the next day, by a bone marrow injection to be administered at home by a nurse, and when she arrived at the house, we saw the face of the future. Because of the virus, she would only meet Deidre – I had to hide in another room with the dog – the house was to be ventilated and she provided a mask for Deidre to wear. We found this interesting rather than inconvenient, and I would have worn a clown suit and cycled across town on a penny-farthing to secure the treatment. The process was completed and we assembled in the kitchen, me wanting to hear how it had gone. Deidre, while looking like she had been punched, expressed gratitude that it was over and she could rest. And rest is what we did.

We cannot be sure if it was the chemo or the bone marrow injection, or neither, but Deidre suffered from extreme tiredness for most of the next week, in addition to aches, pains and a continuing metallic taste, and I was worried that for the first time her resilience appeared to weaken. All of these side effects were to be expected, but they were exhausting her. I began to wonder if we had been naive imagining we were through the worst of it, as, relatively speaking, she had sailed through the first few weeks. We were over the initial shock – as much as anyone ever can be – our nearest and dearest had been informed, and all of a sudden we were at home with time together to plan holidays and other adventures. And already, we were hopelessly in love with Lily.

We would never have chosen this situation in a million years, but when talking about it, it saddened us to think that there are many people dealing with serious illness in much-less-fortunate circumstances. It was a sobering thought, but it drove us on, as despite it all, we still had much to be grateful for.

We endeavoured to keep occupied physically and mentally and to see new value in the lives we would now be leading. It was not easy to get up every morning and be filled with positive thoughts, but there was no alternative and it was still a work in progress. Maybe, just maybe, our lives could remain enriched despite the illness, and we reasoned that at our age nearly everyone is living with one condition or another; indeed, I had drawn comfort from the advice I received that I would probably die *with* COPD rather than *because* of it. We became aware that many of our friends and acquaintances were living with chronic conditions which could not be cured and were on treatment plans for the rest of their lives. Asthma, diabetes, high blood pressure, heart conditions, and others, were afflicting many of our generation simply because we were fighting back and living longer. But it had to be worth it. Life had to be meaningful.

I had developed an obsession for how Deidre must really be coping. For all her outward serenity when we had had a pleasant experience, for example, the boys' visits, after they had left, she was down. Of course, any mother would be at seeing their children leave, but I could not shake off the fear that rather than saying au revoir, to her she was actually saying goodbye to them, that she could never be sure if this time would be the last time. When I pressed her, she assured me that she was doing fine, and for my own sanity, I chose to believe her. Believe her and keep her occupied. And loved.

It took a few weeks, but Deidre's health appeared to be stabilising and everything, in its own way, was looking good. She was not really missing her work, something I feared she could never live without, but with the aid of some colleagues who were also close and loyal friends, she was able to keep in touch with everything while remaining emotionally detached, and as their accounts highlighted the increasing pressure they were under, she knew that her energies had to be saved for other battles.

As a female civil engineer who had to break through the glass ceilings of both the engineering profession and then the civil service, her profession, role and rank gave her much to be proud of, and rightly so. She was universally admired and liked in equal measure and one of only a small percentage of women to be active in the civil engineering profession. But she was very, very good indeed. She was the business.

I can remember, several years ago, accompanying her to Loughborough College in England for a civil engineers' conference. I knew it was a big deal because partners were invited and it was a black-tie or sequinned-dress event. So far so good. The evening passed well. We drank only a little, the meal and entertainment were excellent and, to crown it all, they had thoughtfully laid on an event for the delegates' partners the next morning while the conference itself took place. As this was the home of the famous sports college, I was bursting with anticipation. Next morning came, and after a hearty breakfast I wished Deidre a good conference and headed for the reception area, where we had been told to assemble. There was a large gathering in the foyer, and the noise level was high, but almost immediately, one thing struck me – the partners were all women. I was the only man. Of course.

As we boarded the courtesy bus, I felt the need to make some self-disparaging remarks to the group to confirm that I would be coming too. I began to wonder what feast of delights could possibly have been arranged for this glamorous group, and as there was not a single item of casual wear to be seen, Loughborough College of sporting excellence it would certainly not be.

Unimaginatively, a day's shopping was the treat in store, and luckily for me we alighted at the meeting point of the Leicester City Centre walking tour. I seized this opportunity gratefully, and it was genuinely enlightening, and I even had time for a beverage before the ladies, several hundred shopping bags and I made our way back for dinner. To cap it all, the next day's event, to which both attendees and partners were invited, was a visit to a quarry to witness an explosion. Yes, two people from Northern Ireland being invited to watch an explosion. And they say the Americans don't do irony.

I know that Deidre quietly enjoyed the attention of being such a rare commodity in this environment, and why shouldn't she? Hers was one hell of an achievement, and I was proud of her. I also enjoyed being something of a novelty. But now, sensibly, she was stepping away from the stresses and challenges of her job because her next achievement would be even greater.

But just as we laboured with our new normality, the whole planet was about to be confronted with its own challenge. A new phenomenon appeared as if from nowhere, and as its significance began to dawn on us, we were staring at a potential catastrophe, not only for us, but for the world.

7

People tend to say they remember where they were when, for example, President Kennedy was assassinated, or the planes hit the Twin Towers, or Spurs last won a trophy, but while on 1 January 2020 barely anyone had heard of Covid-19, the corona virus, within a few days in mid-March, hardly anyone hadn't. Covid-19 or SARS-CoV-2, not much when you say them fast. But neither are death or taxes. This virus, coming from China we had heard, was to hit our shores shortly, and there was nothing we could do about it. This virus would be responsible for creating the incoming global pandemic, and we had no idea what it all meant.

I had read that during the 1950s, as the Cold War began to escalate, American science-fiction movies portraying invasions by aliens, most of them hostile, represented a subconscious fear of being invaded by the Soviets and being subjected to communist rule. The 'goodies' always won in the end, of course, but more recent blockbusters, including those whose topic was a contagious disease, were not so reassuring. We gathered around our televisions in a way similar to what my grandparents told me they did with the radio during the Second World War, watching the impending story unfold, speculating on what would and wouldn't be affected. Major events had taken place, including a European Champions League match in Liverpool and a major horse-racing meeting, but many others involving large crowds were being postponed as a precaution. We were finding it almost impossible to comprehend that we were faced with two life-changing occurrences within the space of only seven weeks. Our initial impressions from the news coverage, which was only a couple of weeks old, were that it could be dismissed as something that would pass in a matter of days, without any tangible effect on most of us. But now.

The constant television footage was genuinely frightening. Medical staff were dressed like they were dealing with radioactive fallout, walking about in the wards with large face masks and their bodies covered. The wards themselves were cordoned off with tape and polythene sheeting, adding an eeriness to the whole scene. It was difficult to believe that only a week or so ago I had spent a full day sitting beside Deidre while she received her treatment, reading, looking at my phone, drinking coffee in, despite it being a hospital, a pretty welcoming environment. The staff were highly competent and relaxed and had time for everyone, with the atmosphere conducive to treatment and recovery. The images now in front of our eyes were anything but.

As interest increased to obsessional levels and the

trickle of information became a flow, we were told that while the pandemic began to have an impact late in the 2019–20 financial year, the world's first official lockdown began on the 16 March 2020, with plans for restrictions to be eased only gradually throughout the summer. Various heads of government, including those of the UK and Ireland, appeared on television to address their respective nations, outlining their plans and the stipulations for lockdown, while mere mortals came to terms with a new vocabulary, although death was a word which required no introduction.

To describe the unfolding events as disturbing would not do justice to the events or the collective reaction to them. We were obviously appalled by the early reports of fatalities and of how other countries appeared to be suffering more than our own. But we were also worried about a prospect much closer to home. Hospitals were being overwhelmed by this new breed of patient, and the surge in demand for beds, with only a finite supply, would not only affect those contracting the virus, but would have large knock-on effects on the availability of other types of care provided to the wider population. Without having to discuss it, we had two potential crises: that either of us, as 'vulnerables', would catch the virus, or that Deidre would be denied further cancer treatments.

We scrolled through the emerging statistics seeking assurance that we would be safe, that the virus would have a quick look at us and pass on by. So far it was promising, as evidence gathered from around the world suggested that the virus was affecting specific groups more severely than others, the death rate being much higher among individuals aged seventy and above than among younger individuals, and among men rather than women. Well, Deidre was under seventy and a woman, and I would just have to be extra careful.

The Covid effect became real. To deal with coronavirus cases, the resources available for non-virus patients were already being reduced, and in addition to hospitals delaying or cancelling treatments, it was clear that some patients were postponing appointments or deciding against seeking treatment to avoid visiting a hospital. While understandable, given the panic the coverage of the pandemic had caused, it would store up health problems for the future. Another way to look at it, one favoured by political opposition parties in each country, was that the crows were now coming home to roost, so to speak, as years of neglect and underfunding of health services were beginning to have dire consequences.

The future had never seemed more uncertain, especially to those generations who had not experienced wars, food rationing or any other social hardship, but our future was consumed by Deidre's treatments and, consequently, whether she would continue to live. And for now the world would just have to look after itself.

As if in reaction to the unfolding drama, Deidre endured a week of constant tiredness, and by Wednesday she had succumbed and agreed to relax on the couch during the afternoon, something she had until now resisted, as she thought it would hamper her getting to sleep at night. I suspected she did not want to accept that she was now no longer as energetic as she had been before cancer, a defeat of sorts and something with which I can empathise, as I try to drive myself on in exercise rather than acknowledge that my asthma is getting worse and curtailing my every movement.

We entered the weekend with a trip to collect my asthma prescription twenty-three miles away. It sounds like nothing to get excited about, but the virus was severely restricting travel arrangements. The media gleefully seized upon stories of people who were complaining about missing expensive holidays or facing difficulty getting to their second homes in the country, but, more importantly, real people doing real things were also being curtailed. Children calling with elderly parents, or professional carers making their visits; any kind of meeting was either restricted or prevented. Yes, some people may have their travel arrangements upset, but woopy-do, they could finally reduce their carbon footprint. So says the guy who recently purchased a three-litre diesel vehicle.

We were told the virus had come from wild bats and the first human cases had been identified in Wuhan, China, the previous December. By the end of January, the World Health Organization had described it as a public health emergency, and by 11 March, a pandemic.

As the news intensified and the fireside commentators picked up the pace about the 'Chinese problem', with the inevitable xenophobic references to oriental eating habits and the country's perceived secrecy, it was impossible to underestimate what was happening. Unintentionally feeding this frenzy, Chinese authorities were now 'investigating' anyone who was allegedly spreading misleading information about the outbreak on social media. In their wisdom, the Wuhan City government, where allegedly the virus originated, even held their annual banquet celebrating the Chinese New Year, preparing food at ten different locations for forty thousand families.

The reports of growing numbers of affected people in an increasing number of countries added threat to the warnings from world organisations. While the first recorded death was in January, one month later, the UK government were undecided as to whether outbreaks could be contained by isolation and contact-tracing because many people were infectious despite being asymptomatic. Findings seemed to contradict findings. Recommendations that large meetings should be prohibited were contradicted by reports that such bans would be counterproductive, as they would drive people into huddles and under the radar. No one, as yet, knew, but people were dying.

It was over the period from 10 to 13 March that we really began to take notice, as the Cheltenham Festival, a four-day horse-racing and hat-wearing event, attended by 150,000 people, took place on 10 March. And the following day, Liverpool FC played Atletico Madrid at home, bringing thousands of Spanish fans to the UK. For the first time there appeared to be widespread concern about such large gatherings. Then came the first images from Italy and the total lockdown it had introduced. It was frightening and difficult to take in.

Confused? We were too. As if to continue the toing and froing, we were informed that mass gatherings such as the aforementioned sports events and concerts may have to be cancelled and schools closed for more than two months if the UK were to be badly hit by coronavirus.

Then followed advice warning against greetings such as shaking hands, hugging or any form of contact, leading to the invention of quirks such as elbow-touching – remember my friend the car dealer? The government introduced social distancing measures and the compulsory wearing of face masks in an effort to reduce deaths and peak the levels of the infection.

Drinking in bars, going out to restaurants and coffee shops, sports events, musical and other social occasions were being cancelled or were under threat. And we'd thought missing the Carpenters tribute would be a one-off.

Panic-buying at supermarkets and petrol stations was underway. Abraham Maslow, the famed academic, created a model describing human motivation as a 'Hierarchy of Needs', where survival was fundamental, followed by safety, esteem and 'self-actualisation' as the highest level, where we fulfil our potential, or along those lines. People were now concerned about their survival and food on the table: bread, milk, eggs, wine. All essential. But there was one commodity which almost immediately became more sought after than food or alcohol or, it seemed, life itself: toilet rolls. Bog roll. They were flying off the shelves, although as far as I could discern, diarrhoea was not a symptom of the virus. People, quite obviously, simply need to go to the loo.

We resisted this urge at first, expressing amazement at how gullible people could be and how unedifying their behaviour was as they filled shopping trolleys with everything they could find, including, of course, packet upon packet of toilet rolls. Only a few days after this phenomenon had begun, I had to take Deidre to her GP for a prescription and was amazed at how easily I found a parking space just outside the surgery. As Deidre left the car and entered the building across the road from where I had parked, I noticed what would have been called years ago a 'hard man': shaven head, muscles, T-shirt, tattoos, denims and boots. But this was a very hard man, so hard his arms were shaped like a cowboy's legs and his tattoos were spelt incorrectly. I watched this guy as he crossed the road, ensuring we would not make eye contact as he took a few further strides and entered the local convenience store, or corner shop as they were once called. I assumed, continuing my stereotyping of this gentlemen, that he would emerge with a bottle of fortified wine, even though it was not yet 10.30 in the morning.

Just as my mind was beginning to wander, he appeared again, and to my amazement, he was not carrying a bottle of wine or spirits, or a six-pack of lager. No, this man obviously had his finger on the pulse of supply-and-demand economics. He was carrying the largest box of toilet rolls I think I have ever seen. And they were pink! Luckily, my car windows were closed; otherwise, he might have heard my loud, spontaneous laughter. If I had needed something to cheer me up, I had found it. The story clearly lost something in the retelling, as my account to Deidre received only, "What are you on about?" But it did achieve something. "We need to get toilet rolls," I said with authority, and again she reacted as if I had suggested robbing a bank.

When we need something, it is simple: go online and order it. We had become recent converts, entitled to preferential treatment by the supermarkets because of Deidre's condition, and little did we know how well it would serve us as 'vulnerable people', our new classification. However, many of the shopping websites were displaying the 'No longer in stock' sign against all shapes and sizes of toilet rolls. Concern replaced scepticism as the imagery of our lives without these essential commodities came into focus, and it was not appealing, as neither of us wanted to be that much in touch with nature. The 'hard man' was obviously more perceptive than I had given him credit for. We tried all the major supermarkets which had online ordering facilities to no avail, and when I returned empty-handed from the local Aladdin's cave, known to everyone else as the Post Office, there was a problem.

I know Deidre is taking an issue seriously when she stops asking me to do something and starts doing it herself. However, such was the importance of this project that a compromise was quickly found when we agreed we should both look for the rolls and report back on progress. This was doomed to descend into the usual battle for one-upmanship, but the stakes were high and we browsed the online shopping sites frantically.

After several attempts, we both found a supplier, but

rather than risk losing the purchase and waste time by informing the other, we each pressed the 'Buy now' button and reported our success, anticipating the joy of victory. Unfortunately, there cannot be two winners in this game, so we entered into game number two, 'Recriminations', and this I always lose.

After only a brief flurry of consultation, we decided to keep them all 'just in case', and several days later, the sight of two strong young men carrying about 100 rolls into the driveway provided us with the assurance we needed that we and our bottoms were safe. As I went out to speak to them and take receipt of the precious cargo, we all at least had the decency to laugh. Then a few days later – after our first series of consignments had arrived and secure in the knowledge that with a garage half filled with toilet rolls we could deal with the most extreme of upset stomachs – I had been cutting the grass when a van reversed into the driveway and a young, masked man appeared. We nodded and then he opened the rear doors and lifted our latest order of a fifty-four pack of paper gold dust. As we exchanged glances, I gestured towards the garage door, and when I opened it for him and he saw the stockpile already there, he dropped them and left without a word. That was possibly the worst toilet-roll experience I have ever had, and I've had a few before football grounds became safe for human beings, but beggars could very definitely not be choosers.

For all of this light-heartedness, a more sinister consideration was taking up our thoughts, something even more important than these essentials, something that could not be put at risk; the threat to Deidre being able to continue her treatments appeared to grow. Hospital admissions were continuing to rocket, and news channels were reporting that the National Health Service was in danger of collapse due to what we now referred to as 'Covid-19'.

There is a psychological process for assimilating news: what is the information; what does it mean in terms of understanding it; and what does it mean to me on a personal, practical level? It took no time to get to stage three, as upon hearing the coverage, it became clear that the NHS was under immense strain, and we genuinely feared that Deidre's treatments might be cancelled.

It was unthinkable, but we were thinking it. Now, just as we were coming to terms with our situation, it was unfair that we were ambushed by a new panic. We would know on Thursday, her next appointment, and until then all we could do was watch the drama unfold before our eyes.

But for many, the unthinkable *was* happening. Night after night we were hearing about people dying from the disease, each an unspeakable tragedy. But I had only so much emotional juice, and much as I was upset for them and their families, in my heart of hearts, my only concern was my partner's survival.

Again, action was the best tactic, and Deidre asked to see the oncologist for an answer on whether her treatments could continue. It was Thursday morning, yet another day of reckoning. As we entered the hospital, everything looked normal, but we knew something was different. The staff all seemed to be moving faster along the corridors, looking more serious and with urgency in their expressions. Is this what an impending national disaster looks like? Following a short wait which felt like a lifetime, we met the oncologist, whose expression could be telling us either that we had won the lottery or wouldn't live long enough to make the journey home. If the description 'deadpan' had not been invented, it would be now. But very quickly she conveyed the news we had longed for. Having carried out a risk analysis of Deidre's situation, the danger to her of not continuing the treatments was higher than that to her if she were to catch Covid by visiting the hospital.

The health professionals, again, were brilliant. Their handling of the issue was empathetic and decisive. Obvious as the decision may appear, no one could yet forecast how the virus might affect her immune system, and if it were to be compromised, it would be detrimental to her ability to ingest the drugs, so it had to be a major factor in their deliberations.

Relief does not do justice to our reaction. The decision, however, had one major caveat: if she were to catch the virus, they would suspend the treatments. No pressure then. Her third treatment session was completed, and as the euphoria subsided and I realised how worried she had been, we shed a few tears in the car park. Big boys, and girls, do cry. Before long, however, our joy was tempered by reports that many cancers and other serious cases were being deferred to enable medical staff to deal with the pandemic. We could easily imagine the distress the news would cause to the sufferers and their loved ones, as we had been unable to even contemplate that outcome for Deidre, but although I had only enough energy to look after my immediate family, I could not help my mind wandering back to that cold, dark morning in the waiting room which now seemed so many years ago.

Every three weeks, for six sessions, Deidre would undergo treatments involving chemotherapy and biologicals, administered through a drip, as it is widely referred to, with each treatment preceded by a blood test to ensure that her system was up to it. The procedure lasted most of the day. Given the alternative, this was no sacrifice at all, and we quickly adapted to our new routine. Looking ahead purposefully, we entered the dates faithfully into our respective diaries for as far ahead as seemed practical, clarifying that our final entry was in no way to be interpreted as the 'final entry'.

*

As the declined concert invitation of the previous month and our absence from work meant that we had unwittingly entered our own lockdown, we were now joined by the rest of the country. Through the years, I have found getting to sleep more difficult. Indeed, I would joke that people through their twenties to forties would be obsessed with their sex lives – "Was it good for you, darling?" – and through their fifties and sixties it was their sleep – "How did you sleep? I couldn't get over at all." While, in the years that were left, it was their bowel movements! If I was awake during the night, as I usually was, I would be comforted by the distant sound of light traffic, imagining the exciting things people must be doing to necessitate their having to drive so early in the morning. Perhaps an exotic holiday with connection flights taking them across the world. Important packages containing lifesaving products or luxury items being delivered against a tight deadline. A late return home from an exciting liaison. Each possibility had its own merit.

As I lay there, trying to get back to sleep, the scenarios developed until I marvelled at how the world kept turning and how unimportant each of us was in the scheme of things. My scenarios, naturally, were more exciting than the probable reality that most of the vehicles were carrying minimum-wage service workers home from or to long, exhausting shifts before their whole slog restarted again several hours later. I have always preferred fantasy to reality.

But now. Now when I woke, there was nothing, no sound at all. Not one engine, toot of a horn, change of gear nor roar of acceleration. Nothing. No one was going anywhere, and this was its soundtrack. Luckily, freight vehicles were occasionally continuing to deliver essential items such as food and medical supplies. So far, anyway. How could it happen in this day and age? Some experts wondered, how had it not happened before now? To most of us, the human race had for too long been on a collision course with extinction, bringing animal and plant life with it. Now we had a worldwide contagion looming, and being met only with confusion.

The media's early focus was on the threat to gatherings and large events, and I was comfortable with our agreement not to socialise, as I could see the merits in taking it easy for a while. 'Drink when I'm happy; drink when I'm sad' had been taking a hold again. Virtual yoga would replace vino. As the news about the effects on the health service continued, and no one knew how long this would last, suggesting a later-rather-than-sooner solution, at the back of my mind I could not help worrying that if the situation continued on this trajectory, more than Deidre's treatments would be under threat. Our lifesaving medicines. But that was not for today, so I took a puff of my inhaler and put the kettle on.

Despite everything, the days were beginning to blend. The petrifying shock, the first stage in our journey, had diminished. We seemed to have come to terms with the diagnosis and that we would have to get on with life however it unfolded. We had progressed from wondering if we would make it through the day – or the next day, or the day after that – to an expectation that the next day would come, and then the day after that. And then there was next week to look forward to.

I could not begin to imagine the deepest loss, like that of a child or spouse, nor comment on how they cope, but after my own scare several years ago, and now Deidre's condition, I feel only the desire to get on with life the best we can. I have heard of many people simply giving up without a fight, and while I can understand that, I also understood that for us, this would not be our way. We were not built like that. So as the world was sailing into unchartered seas, given all that had happened, our heads were still above water.

When I sat alone – often in the morning and always with coffee – affirming that it would be a good day, I could not shake off an encroaching sense of unease. It continued to be useful for us to play the game of 'How Lucky We Are' to keep our spirits up. But it caused something else: that old acquaintance, guilt. For all that our situation was bad, and God knows it was bad, I was painfully aware that many people were having to plough on in circumstances much, much worse than our own. They would have cancer or another terminal illness and financial difficulties, young kids or other dependants who do not understand, and demand time and affection. They might be alone, possibly having already lost a loved one, staring at four bare walls. Is it any wonder people give up? I have heard of survivor's guilt, I think they call it, often suffered by the only survivor in a tragedy – a crash, an explosion or an attack. There is no reason to feel guilty any more than we should about all the world's inequalities, but I felt distress for those going through what we were suffering, or worse.

8

Whether it was anything to do with Covid or the impact of her chemotherapy treatments, Deidre had a couple of up-and-down weeks, which, after the steady period, was disappointing. Despite feeling active in the morning, walking the dog and doing things around the house, invariably she fell away by early evening. I could sense her disappointment, but there was nothing I could do.

And just to confirm it, angels do exist, and they walk among us. Those I have seen do not possess wings or long, flowing hair and nightdresses; they simply look like you and me, but they do wonderful things. Conan and Suzanne register as angels in our book, as on their day off, they came to see Mum, bringing food and wine for us. What is remarkable about this is that they were unable to come into the house, meaning that we had to talk to each other through the window, an unworthy welcome after a long journey, and to complete the indignity, they were not even able to use the loo, and to avail themselves of our abundance of toilet rolls.

Fortunately, the weather was pleasant, and there was something of a novelty about the whole experience, and we were able to laugh our way through it. The time was spent comparing notes on lockdown's early days, and as dentists, they were affected more than most. Their tone suggested that they anticipated being in this state for some time, and we joked about how many 'through the window' sessions we could withstand. This was our new world, but despite the obvious inconvenience, Deidre's delight at seeing them was uplifting, and she was always more animated in their company. In the company of angels.

Naturally, shortly after their departure and following a short walk, she flagged in the evening, and due to enjoyment of the visit had an uninterrupted sleep.

The following day the weather was poor, but it allowed her to have a guilt-free, take-it-easy time. Constant tiredness, becoming more pronounced in the evening, now featured regularly in her range of side effects. She appreciated that tiredness was a price worth paying and would have to be managed as an integral part of her life; difficult for a Type A 'get up and go' mother and career woman, but she reasoned that if it became no worse, she would probably take it. We discussed the concept of her saving energy when she did not absolutely need to do something so that it may be used for specific events in which she was genuinely interested. True to form, I bored her with sports analogies, where elite professionals will rest during a game but be ready, vulture-like, for the key moment when they will pounce. Knowing when to stop talking, like knowing when to pounce, was something I needed to work on, but we agreed that tiredness, like wear and tear in the bones, was part of the ageing process, and, in the scheme of things, we were not overly concerned.

It became a process of analysing Deidre's levels of energy, mood and other side effects on a daily basis in an effort to ascertain if there was a trend or anything to help us manage our days during chemo. For all that she would attest to being prepared to put up with nearly anything as long as the treatments were effective – and I would agree with her – it was only human to hope that somehow the effects would reduce to the extent where she could function: sleep, wake, and move without discomfort.

Some days later, she complained that the metallic taste in her mouth was now lingering and was interfering with her appetite. This was not good news. Following my unhelpful enquiry as to whether it was similar to the aftertaste from some alcohol-free lagers, we concluded that it could only have come from the chemo. Not long after, the great arbitrator, social media, confirmed through the testimony of other sufferers that it, indeed, could be one of the side effects of chemotherapy. Unfortunately with social media, it rarely stops with confirmation or otherwise of a fact, but is supplemented by extreme accounts – "The metallic taste gets worse and lingers forever" or causes no end of unthinkable consequences – frightening anyone who reads them. There is bound to be some degree of truth in them, but even though we are drawn to look at them, as when passing the scene of a car crash, they are counterproductive. Deidre's use of social media was none of my business, but it did appear to be a double-edged sword in that it was helpful for her to read accounts of real people going through similar experiences, assuring her that she wasn't alone, but also unhelpful in that, from what she was telling me, none of them appeared to heading for a happy ending.

We discussed this, and in an effort to find a bright side, I fell upon the explanation that people with good-news stories, those who were getting better or already were better, were too busy getting on with their lives and, selfishly, had little motivation to share their stories with others, despite them being the very people she and others needed to hear about. Assuming, of course, they, like angels, exist.

As the weather became quite pleasant in the afternoon, we entered into one of nature's most therapeutic activities by going for a long walk in a forest park only a few miles away, which, as we had hoped, was deserted. Once home, having talked and walked enough for the day, the evening passed uneventfully as my partner succumbed to her tiredness and we went to bed thankful for the day we had just experienced.

When we rose in the morning, as if to demonstrate that my previous day's pep talk on conserving energy for key moments had been totally ignored, Deidre took advantage of the continuing pleasant weather to power wash the entire surround of the house. When I asked why, she clarified that it was something to do. I could not argue with that, as there was not a lot now to do, so I retreated, thankful that her disposition was so positive. The day passed and we had a glass of wine to see in the weekend. Without its little luxuries, life is nothing.

*

My mum likes to keep it simple. She always has. I have probably noticed this more since my dad passed, having been exposed more to her habits as we try to assist in whatever we can in these last, lonely years of her life. For her, things are never simpler than in matters of faith. It was always the same, and if there is a heaven, my mum will be up there with a gold star, making sure everyone has the correct prescription. Social conditioning – where youse were brung up – of course, had much to do with it but, her own parents were no 'Holy Joes' for most of their lives. Somewhere along the way, total acceptance and certainty about things which cannot be seen became the guiding posts for her life. Please do not get me wrong, I am delighted, and I said many times that even if there is no man – she would see God as a man – sitting on a cloud with someone playing a harp and ladies with wings, the lifestyle and happiness faith gave my parents was reward in itself for them and thrilling to observe, so no argument from me, only, at times, envy.

She manages to dissect events, identifying where a good thing happened to prove not only God's existence, but his love for us all. The old story about missionaries smuggling bibles into communist countries – where the bibles were left highly visible in the back seat of the car but remained undetected by the customs guards – or the person cured from cancer through prayer is, to her, irrefutable evidence.

This particular morning when I called her to check in and hear about her legs, visits to the loo during the night, contact from friends or fraudsters trying to fool her into giving away her fortune and what's on television, I was less that enthused about having to report that Deidre was not so good. As the conversation developed – in our terms, beyond thirty seconds – I felt the need to soften the blow by emphasising how, in the big picture, she was doing well and keeping her spirits up. My mum replied by affirming that her prayers and those of the congregation in her church were being dedicated to Deidre and that she was in God's hands. I couldn't resist, and before I could catch myself on, I had reacted with the, "Well, wouldn't it have been better if God hadn't given her the cancer in the first place? Then none of this would be happening to us." Out it came.

"I know, Son, I know."

"Well, here's hoping," was the only closure I could think of.

My mum asked me to pass on her love to Deidre and the boys and then she was gone. I set my phone down and immediately bitterly regretted what had just taken place. I was, quite simply, out of order.

After making a mess of my call to my mum, I returned to Deidre, who confirmed that she was feeling very up and down, and tired. When she is feeling good, it is easy to relax and make believe that nothing is wrong, even for a while. But mornings like this bring it home, and when the realisation returns, fear follows. I am frightened, every minute of every day, but the challenge is to keep it hidden or disguised.

As we woke on Sunday morning, Deidre had settled again, and we enjoyed a slow, quiet day with the newspapers, just what Sundays were for. Monday, Tuesday and Wednesday continued the rollercoaster of 'good/bad' days, but through it all, she was a tower of strength. That she could deal with such an up-and-down experience, both physically and emotionally, would serve her well as she continued her treatments and her refusal to be defined by her condition. Thursday introduced some excitement as we made the twenty-mile journey to collect my prescription from the chemist. While doing so, I was forced to consider my own condition, and so far I had not been overly troubled by Lily's presence, and for that I was also grateful. But I would be on asthma inhalers for the rest of my life and I had come to see them as an ally rather than something be embarrassed about. As we travelled, I only had to look to my left to appreciate that they were no inconvenience at all.

Too good to be true. There was no better way of describing it. I knew I was awake, because I could see the ceiling and I could feel the faint breeze coming through the window. But after that... I could not move and I could not breathe. There was an invisible lump of concrete positioned on my chest. I realised that the dog may be hypo-allergenic, but I was obviously allergic to hypo-allergenic dogs. It had taken a few weeks, but it had come, big time. I eased myself up and, once I had sat up, reached for my inhaler. A double dose today. I began playing my mental video presentation entitled 'How Could I Have Been So Stupid?', starring Lily and myself, with scenes of me with the pup on my knee, on my chest, in my arms, resting on my foot, and so on. Everywhere she shouldn't have been. I imagined my next appointment with my doctor.

How is your asthma behaving, Colin?

I got a dog.

What? Why didn't you just walk in front of a bus? It will have the same effect.

I started moving but was wheezing terribly. This was not good. I remembered that my time in enclosed spaces with the dog had been much higher than anticipated, as I was not at work, nor going out a lot due to lockdown, so through changed circumstances, I had brought it on myself. I had taken to wearing a snood and gloves when feeding and walking Lily first thing in the morning, which, apart from scaring the neighbours, was clearly ineffective. What now? We had a healthy supply of face masks in case we ever went out again, and plenty of toilet rolls for that matter, but I needed something more radical. I called my health centre for help, and thirty minutes later I was still calling my health centre. Luckily, I had nowhere to be! Eventually, I was given the opportunity to leave a message, which I did, and that afternoon I received a call from the asthma nurse, as I entitled her.

"I need your help. My partner has cancer and we got a dog and I am allergic to the dog even though it is meant to be hypo-allergenic, but because we haven't been able to go out, I am with her even more, and I have to take her out in the morning for a walk, and I can't breathe," to which she would probably have been thinking that I cannot breathe because I talk too much. But fortunately, she was still on the line and did not chastise me as I had anticipated.

"The only thing to do is have at least one room where the dog never goes," and I grunted my agreement. "Also, are you taking antihistamines?"

"I tried them, but they made me very sleepy. You see, my partner's mum has a dog, and I used to take them when I was going down there..." I realised she did not need to hear this, as her time was precious.

"There are new ones you can get which do not make you drowsy. We can get you those," and I was encouraged. At last, the elusive cure for this God-awful condition. "Also, you can use your blue inhaler as often as you need." I did not know this.

"Oh, I didn't know that. I thought it was only four times a day," I offered as if I had been keeping my intake at that level.

"That's for asthmatics, but you have COPD," not all good news then, "and you can use it more often." Fair enough.

That evening I commenced my self-imposed exile in the other room, and it wasn't all bad, as I was able to catch up on the programmes I like to watch – spies, guns, car chases, all that uplifting stuff, but it was good fun and I began to breathe again. It was a 'no cure, no solution' dilemma, as the dog was going nowhere. But as the next instalment of the box set began to run, I took a puff of my inhaler and decided that those decisions could wait for another day.

On Friday, after my excitement of the previous twenty-four hours, we were able to re-focus on Deidre, who was suffering from sore legs and an itch. There are few things worse than an itch you can't scratch, and at least one of her fellow social media sufferers had confirmed that this side effect in particular had caused some people to cease their treatments, so bad had it become.

When I asked her if she could ever foresee herself doing similar, giving up, she responded, as I expected, that she could not, and, at least, that was something. So distressing was it to see her in so much discomfort, for the first time I took on my own Internet project to find a solution. I worked on the basis that if we could reduce the side effects, the treatments themselves would be manageable. Good in theory. I wanted to learn about it, challenge it and, ultimately, defeat it in the same way I wanted to with asthma. But like asthma, we would not win the war, and we could hope only to triumph in a series of daily battles. For some, it would be no way to exist, but for us, it was the only way we could live.

On Saturday, when Conan and Suzanne visited again, they brought sunshine and wonderful news for a soon-to-be grandmother. Short of a cure, this was the best thing she could hope to hear. In their own inimitable way, they produced an X-ray photograph of the baby inside a card for Deidre. I still remember my own mother's joy when she heard similar news from my brother many years ago, but Deidre's reaction easily exceeded it on the decibel scale. They had kept it all very quiet, and looking back, although there were telltale signs, the surprise served to heighten the joy. Well done, you two, and even the dog was delighted.

The rest of the day was spent discussing all aspects of baby, and as we were sitting outside due to the continued restrictions, I happily assumed my role as chef and waiter, covering two separate tables. While it was obviously a terrible situation, there was something hilarious about us sitting several feet apart shouting our questions and answers.

As they were departing, I noticed a tear in Deidre's eye. Was it of joy or sadness? I did not know but did not want to ask. I could imagine. Somewhere behind the joy of the arrival of a grandchild, there must have been the thought of how long she would have to see the baby grow, take first steps, go to school, college, get married and make her a great-grandmother. *If only*, I thought. But this was an occasion when Deidre was entitled to her own private reflections. After a while, when I enquired as to how she enjoyed the afternoon – no more than that – she admitted allowing her mind to wander to how many years she would be around to see her grandchild grow up. Every prospective grandparent must have felt that, but fewer had such a shadow hanging over them. I did not offer a positive slant on what she told me. I did not, because I could not, and we were back to wondering how long she would live.

*

The conversation began, and probably for the first time, we gave some thought to the longer term future, something I had been wary of bringing up, even now. Deidre continued, understandably, to express the view that we should live one day at a time as, in reality, that was all we could do.

"I know why you are saying that, but I still think you can. I think you can and you should. *We* should. Really," I countered, trying to sound reasonable but treading cautiously.

"We don't know what will happen."

"But no one knows what will happen," I responded, and although this statement is factually true, even *I* was irritated by it.

"It is possible that in time the treatments will fail and I will go backwards. That's what can happen. They don't necessarily work forever. Then I will be on chemo again and unable to do anything. All over again." Just right now I had no comeback. I was also tired, and my motivational speeches had deserted me. We sat in silence for what seemed like a lifetime.

"We don't know that that is going to happen. But you are a winner, and you will win this too. There is absolutely no reason why we cannot plan ahead. In fact, I think it is exactly what we should do." I was finding some momentum at last.

"Planning ahead makes me have to think about what is going to happen... and that's not something I'm able to do right now," she explained, quite reasonably.

I understood. While we had broached the subject and, inevitably, had our own thoughts, we had not discussed how long she had. Not really. It was too painful, but now it was the conversation we needed to have. I do not believe in predestination or that our days are counted. I believe there are things we do, both positively or negatively, to prolong or shorten our time above ground. Through good fortune or misfortune, we can be in the right or wrong place at the right or wrong time – plane crashes, car accidents, and the like. Where does cancer fit into this sense of logic? Is it brought upon oneself by what we do or neglect to do? Is it predetermined by our genes or is it simply bad luck? I do not know. And establishing how and why she contracted this abominable thing would be of academic interest only. We know there is no cure and that she will be on medicine and drugs for the rest of her life. But many people are in a similar position, and the happy ones maintain their focus, not only on the duration but also on the quality of life, and I believe they are rewarded. Easy for me to say, and I hoped she agreed.

Having had the discussion which would settle us for a while, the next few days passed uneventfully, and she was in good spirits as thoughts of the first grandchild sank in. They may have been uneventful days, but they were the days which made our lives worthwhile. To simply relax, take our time over things and be glad we were here. When this journey began, these were the days we were aiming for, and now, give or take a wobble or two, we had hit the target. Not only were we alive, but we were living.

By Wednesday, as Deidre prepared for her scan and fourth treatment on consecutive days, she was apprehensive. If the treatments were like the study, the scans were the exam results. They would show progress, or otherwise, and dictate the mood for our lives until the next one. The day did not start well, as Deidre woke up with sore legs. While this told us nothing in terms of the scan's outcome, we would have preferred her preparations to have been uncomplicated. There was a lot riding on this. If the scan results were good, it was possible that the biological treatments could replace chemotherapy. The hope for success was matched by the fear of failure. Affirmations, prayers, the lot. And then to wait.

Neither of us slept that evening, mulling over the possibilities and improbabilities, so by Thursday morning, neither of us looked ready for the catwalk. But there was a big day ahead, and early on we had good news. As well as receiving her fourth treatment, Deidre's liver results had improved immensely, and the oncologist stated that she was optimistic about the general success of the Perjeta treatment Deidre would be receiving. Words are interpreted and carry weight, so the word 'positive' scores highly coming from a medical professional and was exactly what we needed to hear. I could see the spring in my partner's step, and it gave me a nice warm feeling.

As we entered week twelve, despite a poor night's sleep, we were excited in anticipation of the new lockdown phenomenon, the Zoom quiz. For people our age, this involved great feats of technology, where we linked with each other on screen through an app called Zoom with almost no time delay or loss of connection. I had to 'unlock' my laptop to bring Zoom into the system, achieved with much less difficulty than I had feared, leaving me very pleased with myself. So much so, that I decided not to announce that I had done it but instead, in the spirit of reverse attention seeking, when asked if I had achieved it, would affect nonchalance as if it was something I did regularly and with ease.

"Did you manage to sort that unlocking thing out, because you know we need to if we want to do this quiz?" I was asked.

"Yes," I answered, allowing that one word to resonate. I was delighted that Zoom has the visual facility because although nothing was said, the expressions, either of surprise or disbelief, were priceless.

Once Deidre had her injection out of the way, we were able to commit to the serious business of preparing for the quiz. Four other couples were to join in, with Conan and Suzanne acting as hosts and question masters. This was a relief, as while Deidre and I had set the evening up, we were depending on Conan, who was conversant with the technology and could 'troubleshoot' if necessary, to deliver the goods. The hosts' questions covered a range of categories and the quiz was long enough to be engaging without becoming boring, and while I cannot remember the scores, just for the record, we won. The real winner, however, was the evening itself.

It was a novelty to 'meet' our friends in such unforeseen circumstances, but we were simply happy to be talking with people, as socialising had been so abruptly but necessarily snatched from us. I know Deidre really enjoyed the evening, and it did no harm that the others were so complimentary about her new look.

Some say looks do not matter, and I understand what they mean. But looks can matter very much. They can matter for many people in various circumstances, and Deidre was a prime example. Her appearance was a measure of how she was managing her terrible disease, and this kind of feedback was a tonic. It had been a Good Friday indeed. Saturday maintained the vibes, and we erected the patio furniture in the sunshine which had been delivered 'despite Brexit', while our next-door neighbour left us a delicious cake. She could win any bake-off! Despite itchy legs later in the evening, it had been a very satisfying weekend so far.

*

One of the many sayings I remember from childhood is '*The Lord giveth and the Lord taketh away*'. Strictly speaking, it seems to mean that the Lord gives you something and then takes it back again, a bit like the government, only in the case of the latter, they take more than they give. Whatever it is meant to mean, it seemed to fit with our emerging pattern, as, inevitably, a few good days were followed by a few difficult ones.

Easter Sunday was always going to be awkward, as, second only to Christmas Day, it was the biggest family occasion, with a three-line whip in operation for boys, mother and associates. But this year it would not take place. The pandemic had put paid to that. No one would be travelling due to the strict rules still in place for meeting in houses, family or not. This edict, however, saved us from a potentially distressing situation. I feared that Deidre, even with all the assistance we could provide, would not have enough energy to host such a gathering given the pressure she puts herself under to make things perfect. We could blame the government's rules, the pandemic, the Chinese (if you are an American president) or the Lord for giving and then taking away, but we did not have to come face-to-face with potential failure.

We more than made up for our inability to meet with a series of telephone and WhatsApp calls, and as the two of us were enjoying our meal that evening, she intimated that as she had been tired and achy all day, she would have been unable to host dinner, so we laughed and concluded that maybe what had happened was, in its own way, a good thing. Sometimes having a choice is overrated.

9

Easter Monday and Tuesday passed with no change, and by Wednesday, as it was such a lovely day, we ventured out with the dog for a long walk, which did the heart and soul good. Others were out, but we all kept our distance. It was like a zombie science fiction movie, but without the fiction.

Thursday was the biggest of days. Scan results day. The butterflies were flapping furiously in my stomach, and as for Deidre, while she displayed the demeanour of someone heading into town for some shopping, she could only have been in turmoil. This was the big one. All future tests would be rendered meaningless if we did not get a result today. No pressure at all.

Due to the Covid restrictions, I was not permitted to attend, so when she left, I waved her goodbye as if she was heading to her first day at school. Now it was out of our hands. A few more prayers, promises to be a better person if this all worked out, and then the wait. I pictured where she would be every few minutes: in the car park, entering the building, reception, the waiting room, and then the call from a nurse. Would the nurse's expression give anything away? Did the nurse even know anything? The wait. When waiting in circumstances like this, any activity, no matter how valuable in its own right, is simply a means of passing time. A distraction. And I had several distractions. My CD collection – yes, I still play them in the car – was rearranged into alphabetical order, the updated list of books I had read since January, the dishwasher was emptied and restocked, and I ironed a batch of white T-shirts; not well, but they were to go under sweatshirts and pullovers, so it didn't matter if they had creases. Right now, I couldn't think of anything that mattered less.

At last I noticed her car enter the driveway, and I immediately retreated to the kitchen. I did not want to be waiting anxiously at the door but hoped to present as casual a facade as I possibly could. I anticipated that Deidre's expression would tell me nothing. As she came into the kitchen, neither of us spoke, but when she smiled, I smiled too. I walked to her and gave her a big hug. I was aching to hear the results, but if they were bad, I needed this moment to last forever. I set her down and stepped back, as I sensed she wanted space. She cleared her throat and spoke. "Significant regression in all tumours: breast, 7.5mm to 3mm; right lung top, 8mm to 3mm; right lung bottom, 10mm to 4mm; and liver, 5.5cm x 6.5 to 4cm x 0.8cm. Delighted!"

It was like passing every exam or being pronounced innocent of all charges.

"So that's what they told you?" as if I didn't believe. I barely dared believe it.

"Yes, the oncologist was very pleased." *Very pleased? Very pleased? I'm so pleased I could kiss next door's cat!* While Deidre maintained an outer aura of calm, I was delirious. Was it positive thinking, affirmations, prayer or cosmic ordering? Was it all of these? Or none of these? But just at that moment I neither knew nor cared. The doctor said, all that time ago, that we had a chance, and here we were, taking it. There was a long road ahead, but we were going in the right direction and the first step was a good one. And then some.

"Hello, Miss Twelve Per Cent," I said, and Deidre, beaming, knew what I meant.

The importance of this scan result could not be underestimated. It was like a validation of our positive approach, our belief that we could in some small way define Deidre's own future rather than lie down and accept defeat. We didn't notice the time passing, but this was one of the best days of our lives.

As we entered week thirteen, the good feelings and energy generated by the scan result continued and we took a long walk on the beach, again at Moville, and through its adjoining village. The simplest things in life were the most beautiful, and the sun was bright, the breeze fresh and the day clear. Deidre tired later in the evening and complained about the metallic taste in her mouth returning, but, for now, we were unconcerned. We had that set of results on our side. *Yes, Mr Specialist, we do have a chance.*

The following week alternated between Deidre feeling good and active and being tired and lethargic, but we were able to continue with the walks, which were so necessary, and even a barbecue. Active, rest, active, rest, if it was to become our pattern, was one we could live with. A further sign of progression was the resumption of household projects, and the hot press was first in line for a reboot, as it clearly hadn't been painted in a while. After receiving my instructions, I decided that the best way to complete the mission was to do it on my own rather than do it on my own with constant supervision and critique. A decent job was done – eight out of ten was the feedback – but we were progressing, and that was all that mattered. When Deidre was thinking about jobs to be done, she was not dwelling on her condition.

On Friday, after another exhilarating walk, we decided to stimulate our brain cells that evening with another Zoom quiz, which, although for the record we were not victorious, was still great fun. It was heartening to see everyone enjoying themselves, and the post-quiz conversation reminded us that everyone is dealing with problems of one kind or another. They are part of being alive.

It was Saturday. I knew that because the day and date say said it on my phone. Puppy walked, peeped and pooped, and now, thankfully, quiet. The spare computer cable that nobody claimed ownership of finally came in handy as she jumped, chased and pounced on its every swing from my hand. And the sun was even trying to break through. It was the weekend, and they were meant to feel different, they always did. For a start, there was no work, at least after I gave up my Saturday job forty years ago, when I took my first weekend off.

But I can remember that they felt different before there was work, even when I was at school there was that feeling. Perhaps the differences were that we didn't have to get up early, though on a Saturday we didn't feel tired, and Mum and Dad told me to go back to bed, as they had things to talk about. This always had me worried. Were they going to sell me to the gypsies like that other bad boy Mum told me about, the one who wouldn't tidy his room and be nice to his little brother? Or were they going to fall out like Kevin's mum and dad were doing? I knew this because I had heard them talking about it. I really hoped Kevin's mum and dad wouldn't fall out, as although no one seemed to like him – my mum told me not to go anywhere on my own with him – I wanted to be his friend and he taught me how to do things.

For years Saturday meant an early taxi home from wherever I had been the night before, hangovers and sport, watching or playing, and as I think back, I didn't seem to fear the approach of Monday morning as much as I had come to. Saturdays were different. Even on holidays, in different time zones, they were different, and it was generally agreed that that was a good thing. "It breaks up the week," my mum would say, and we would all nod knowingly in agreement, although to this day I am not sure what she meant. But what about now? It used to be that each day brought something a little different with it: the plans to eat, drink and spend less; the middle period where, hopefully, the television was good; or the growing anticipation of the forthcoming weekend with its fun, surprises and sport, at least until late Saturday night when I didn't want to go to bed because that would signify the official end of the fun and the creeping fear of the new Monday.

Now? It was difficult, no matter how I tried to differentiate one day from another. I read and listened to the news, but that had become one long virus report. Did the weekends feel like anything any more? Did anything feel like anything any more?

Reality, thankfully on this occasion, bit again during the week as Deidre had her bloods done, to ensure she was not reacting negatively to her treatments. In the scheme of things, this is a minor hurdle to jump but it must be completed successfully or 'we do not pass go'.

In an attempt to 'pass go', Deidre continued chemotherapy and biological treatments on Thursday. They must work, and work quickly, as despite the fact that they are used to remove cancerous cells, long term they can damage the body. Without saying anything, we were both aware of what was at stake. Yet again. A quiet prayer was said, and I could only trust it would be rewarded. By the end of week fourteen she had completed five treatments. It was a remarkable achievement for her and her medical professionals, but sadly, for many others, their progress did not follow a similar trajectory.

The pattern of good sleep, bad sleep continued, and we were unable to identify anything more specific than the general effects of the treatments as to why. Naturally, Deidre's morale would be influenced by the quality of her rest, and it made life like trying to walk on two treadmills at the same time, each moving at a different speed. One, representing life under lockdown, was slow, simple and repetitive. The other, our lives with cancer, was up and down, and changed speeds at random. As least we were not bored, as many must have been. The metallic taste was becoming a more regular feature, and she had already established, through social media, that this was a common side effect but one which may disappear through time. Here's hoping. There was still a battle to persuade her to rest during the day when she felt tired, even though I understood her rationale for preferring to remain active. Thankfully, we were able to take walks, which were good for our minds as well as our bodies.

It was Monday, 18 May. My alarm went off at 7.20 and I rose immediately, took my inhaler and tablet, and washed and dressed quickly. I entered another bedroom, where I had left the kettle the previous evening along with my coffee mug to ensure a minimum of noise which might wake the pup. The operation was executed with precise timing and finesse, and within ten minutes total, the Cayenne was reversing down the driveway, its journey underway. I took one final glance into the back seat to ensure my packages were secure and I turned onto the street. Although the traffic seemed to have increased from previous weeks, it was still non-existent by normal standards, and as I entered the main road, I granted myself a light chuckle as the mission was going smoothly and was likely to be successful. As I negotiated the main roundabout and found the outside lane without difficulty, I couldn't help but be a little apprehensive as to what I might find as I rounded the slight bend as the road dipped towards the river which divides the city in more ways than one. Within two minutes I had arrived, and as there were no hostiles evident, I made the right turn, ready to execute my mission.

The council dump was open again and I joined the queue. I had left nothing to chance. Such was the clamour to lose all our rubbish and the fear of contagion with so many people in close contact, council staff had been severely restricting the numbers permitted to enter, and many people, so we heard, were being turned away. As well as my flask of coffee, I had my book and the previous day's Sunday Times travel section, and, of course the local radio was providing updates on dump activity in the region. I took my time, remembering there was no rush – *Don't do anything to blow it now!* – and I even risked a brief chat with one of the attendants, complimenting him on how well the site had been set up to deal with long queues of cars which formed a snake in the immediate area. Progress was slow but sure, and as each minute passed, I became increasingly confident of success. I was directed into the fourth of four shorter lines, and my sense of anticipation rose accordingly. *Not long now.* The sequencing of the cars from lines one to four was unclear, and I was not at all confident that the attendant in charge of this crucial function was on top of his brief: stay in 'drive mode' with the footbrake on, to be released the second I received the vital nod. It would be the worst time to be distracted and lose my slot. Then the moment arrived. The car in line two took its place to enter the gates next. There was room for two cars, however, and immediately, like a predator with its prey, I took my chance with a swift release of the brake, a press of the accelerator and a left turn. I was in position now, and no one could stop me. I inadvertently made eye contact with the attendant, a schoolboy error. I thought, but he quickly looked away – something else had attracted his attention – and my engine revved up as if in acknowledgement of passing the gates. I followed the next attendant's directions with a smile, and before I could say "Vodka Martini, shaken not stirred", I was leaving the premises, cardboard, wood, grass and general rubbish deposited.

Mission accomplished, I returned home in triumph – having taken only one hour – to recount the highlights of my adventure, complete with cars, crowds, attendants and rubbish. A couple of hours later, as we followed the same route to take a walk across the bridge, I suggested we should look to see how many cars were stuck in the queue or being turned away in failure as they were not blessed with my amazing gift of foresight. When I asked Deidre to count how many cars were backed up as we passed the dump, she said, "None." Not the answer I expected, and as I could not resist a peek myself, I could see that not one single vehicle was in that queue.

"They must have closed," I ventured.

"Nope, they are wide open," was the crushing response.

"Well, I don't know; it was choc-a-bloc when I was down earlier." Deidre gave me a look which suggested that she thought I might have sloped off somewhere, except there was absolutely nowhere to go.

*

On 24 January, Deidre received a diagnosis of Stage 4 breast cancer which had spread to her liver and lungs. On 4 and 5 February she underwent her first chemo and biological treatments, and today, 21 May, she was attending hospital for her sixth and final chemo treatment of this session. And she will remain on biological treatments for as long as they continue to work.

It's not a lot when you say it quickly, but what a remarkable journey she has undertaken in such a short time. For those who say positivity does not work, I will not try to convince you otherwise. But what I do know is that I see it every day in various guises. In every message there is the content and process: the message and the manner in which the message is delivered, and in conversation, the process can be the tone and emphasis. When she left the hospital following her morning consultation, which confirmed that she would be having treatment that afternoon, she had a metaphorical spring in her step. That spring came from the conversation with yet another oncologist. In relating the details, it was clear that this gentleman is not only a competent medical professional but a skilled communicator.

While he used the term "I cannot promise anything",

he was providing realistic hope, thus lifting her spirits and making her even more determined to survive and prosper. He gave her a fighting chance because he described it as a chronic condition as opposed to a terminal illness. He wasn't even saying anything different to others she had spoken with, but it was all in the 'how', and, by God, *how* he managed to do that.

Although this was, hopefully, the final chemo treatment, we were by no means out of the woods yet, and the injection was to be given the following day, with the side effects destined to reintroduce themselves like unwanted relatives at your child's wedding. But as we looked back and reflected on this short but traumatic period of nearly four months, we could afford to look forward with belief and more than a little expectation.

Many years ago, to my family's consternation, I became a punk rocker. To them, all of a sudden, David Bowie was quite normal. The movement grew out of frustration with everything – the government, lack of career opportunities, frequent strikes – and it fostered a distinctive look, fashion and attitude based largely on nihilism, or 'no future', as the catchphrase became. It also spawned a quasi-political dimension, often nourished by the music press, which had grand ideas about its own importance. As is usually the case, those with talent went on to become part of music's mainstream, the people they opposed originally, having used punk as a vehicle to gain attention.

For me, sure I wanted killings and bombings in my homeland to end, but by this stage in my life I was into music, football, girls, my looks, alcohol and lagging far behind in my studies. Pop music had become elitist, distant and appeared to have pulled the corporate ladder up behind itself, meaning only those with sufficient resources and backing would have even the remotest chance of making it. Punk, if only for a short time, changed this. I was into the music, nothing more fanciful, and the opportunities it provided for kids like myself with no money or experience, bad instruments and, to be honest, precious little talent, to 'form a band'. And almost overnight, many of us did. This experience resonated with me again because of one key factor, the punk movement grew quickly from nothing throughout several countries and built a momentum all of its own. It was not manipulated, and it could not be stopped. In its early stages anyway. Something similar was happening now.

People everywhere were coming out of their houses at the same time on a Thursday evening to applaud the staff of the National Health Service. From towns and villages, middle-class developments and working-class streets, people of all ages, creeds and vocations emerged to show their gratitude. There appeared to be little organisation centrally, and it was embraced through word of mouth and, of course, social media. Another example of a good idea well publicised, and, again, this had grown from the people and it was wonderful. The sincerity of the gratitude expressed was moving. Neighbours were talking – from a distance, naturally – some for the first time, and it was a genuinely warm atmosphere. It was no more than a gesture; it would not put bread on the table of harassed, overworked health service workers. We accepted that as an altogether different matter, but I hope they saw it for what it was. We were saying "Thanks", and believe me, our gratitude was deep.

We had every reason to be grateful. Deidre's treatments were continuing and progressing as well as they possibly could. Not for the first time, I thought of the people I had met in the waiting room that morning and hoped that their treatment plans had not suffered because of Covid. And not for the first time either, I admitted to myself that I had only enough emotional juice for what I was directly dealing with, but I knew how lucky we had been. I was smart enough but not too proud to know that.

Another big day had arrived in our new world: the day in which we would host the evening quiz. Despite the steroids, Deidre had slept well and gave us both a lift by confirming that she was feeling good, as the day would be devoted to ensuring that every detail of preparation was attended to. The plan was complex and I went over each task at least twice. We had landed people on the moon, taken photographs of Mars – *sorry, Bowie, there is no life* – and transplanted hearts and other organs, and hosting this quiz without incident would be up there with those achievements. I enjoyed taking part and, occasionally, winning, but I quite fancied myself as a quizmaster. Maybe it was the power. Or perhaps the trend of quizmasters making sarcastic comments to the contestants at the end of each round. Probably both. Hosting the quizzes also played to Deidre's strengths, as she devised various ways to keep a running score and ensure there was no cheating.

Needless to say, it went swimmingly, with most couples being in contention until the last round, the sign of a good quiz in my book. That was until I knocked a glass of red wine over my laptop. There is not much that makes you look and feel more foolish than spilling a drink everywhere. However, we said our goodbyes and mopped up in private.

The week continued the pattern of good sleep, bad sleep, metallic taste, walk, and good sleep again. This was normal life: walking the dog, resting, and quizzes on Zoom media, including my friend Paul, in Cork, and his wife's family, and even a bit of virtual yoga. We were adapting to our personal circumstances, but also to those of the world which had changed unrecognisably.

Sadly, Deidre noticed that her nails appeared to be loosening, a common side effect but one we hoped to have avoided. However, to counterbalance this, she reported that the dreaded metallic taste was weakening. Brilliant, and something to focus on if her nails did, indeed, weaken further. Perhaps the Lord does give and also take away in equal measure after all. All in all, a good week, as weeks go.

*

I think back frequently to the people I came across that morning at the cancer ward: the women trying to deal with their diagnoses, and their partners dealing also with the shock and sense of helplessness. Where are they now, and how are they faring? Have some of them passed away already? Hopefully not, but in this world anything is possible. It is harrowing to realise that every minute of every day of every year, people are hearing the news that they have cancer. For some there is a long battle ahead, and for others, tragically, they are barely given the time to say their goodbyes.

There are many cancers and many treatments, and for certain types, massive progress has been made. We should all be grateful and hopeful that similar developments are made in the cancers which remain, darkly, categorised as a 'death sentence'. Sufferers and their loved ones will deal with the situation in different ways. Some will face adversity head on, some even benefitting from telling the world of their struggles, and social media has been a useful tool in this approach; others remain more private, dealing with their situation in a quieter and, what I imagine for them, more dignified way; and there will be people who, faced with the immensity of it all, will continue as if it is not happening; and, sadly, some people will simply fold. I am not here to judge, and I am a great believer in whatever gets you there is good, but I do hope that every sufferer has at least one person with whom they can share their time, their feelings, their fears and, quite simply, their presence.

Because of that day and the profound affect it had on me as a partner, I feel a sense of affinity with those poor souls I shared a waiting room with that cold, bleak Monday morning, even though I know nothing about them except for one fact. Cancer sufferers and partners, we are on the same journey together. We will, inevitably, take different directions, and there will be different outcomes, many unthinkable, but such is the reality of life. And, unfortunately, death. While thinking through the events of that morning causes me to relive the trauma, I cannot help but do so, as I wish them well, and in doing so, I reflect, yet again, on our own circumstances and take comfort in the belief that for all the pain we have experienced, we are truly blessed.

10

We have entered the twentieth week of our own lockdown. Again, not long in the scheme of things, and like many of these phenomena, it feels both like a lifetime and a split second all in one go. We had a very useful conversation about how far we have come and how well we, individually and as a couple, have dealt with the situation. I am relieved to hear this because, at times, I do have my doubts about how I am managing. Am I doing enough? Am I being positive enough? Am I too selfish, perhaps for Zooming my friends or having an additional glass of wine? I do not know, but talking about it is helpful.

After the spirit-lifting sunshine and heat of last week, today is unpleasant and autumnal. I somehow managed to avoid the rain during Lily's early morning walk and was able to converse with the members of the unofficial dog-walking club which I now seem to have joined. It's a pleasure, as they are all lovely people. Me saying dog-walkers being lovely people? Times have definitely changed.

Following my successful adventure at the local council dump on the Glendermott Road, it closed for no apparent, hopefully *despite* rather than *because* of my mission. Officially, it was too small to hold people safely, and other businesses which were still permitted to operate in the immediate area had complained about the disruption caused by the queues. A new mission, should I decide to accept it, was to successfully proceed to the council dump in Claudy, about ten miles away, just off the road to Belfast. This was a welcome challenge but one which, it was decreed, we would accomplish together. Oh well.

As I drove, Deidre made her usual morning calls, and I was lost in my thoughts until I realised I had no idea where we were going. At this stage, we tend to play the game of 'decipher the hand sign or decode the mumble', the hand sign being either left, right, straight ahead or somewhere, while the sound simply frightens the dog. But neither helps me. I need to learn to use the satnav.

When we arrived at our destination, we were met by an earnest-looking man who appeared intent upon getting right up close to me, too close for these days, and while Deidre ordered me not to open the car window, that was the only course of action available. It was when he came close enough to give me a sexually transmitted disease, never mind the virus, that I spoke up and used the Vulcan death stare to signal that enough was enough.

"What have you got?" Today was not the day for smart-ass answers either.

"A chair and some cardboard," which effectively translated into, "Nothing at all really. Sorry for wasting your time, but if you knew how bored I was becoming, you would understand."

"A chair and some cardboard," he shouted to a colleague who was out of sight.

"That's okay," came the reply from unseen man, followed up by, "That's okay," from our too-close-for-comfort friend. "The chair goes into plastics," – I had mentioned that it was a plastic chair at the time our application for admission was being considered – "and the cardboard is on round."

In we went, and after I had put on the brakes, opened the boot and removed the chair, the previously unseen man appeared to tell me that the chair should be despatched at furniture and to keep to the right. I successfully followed the instructions, and we dispatched our load and drove off into the wet, unwelcoming morning. This mission was definitely less exciting than the previous one, but it did pass some time. The newspaper was acquired, and we were back to continue our morning routine, whatever that was. For me, exercise and breakfast, which had become brunch, would get me through until early afternoon, and then some writing.

A trip to the cottage provided a welcome change even though we were unable to meet Deidre's family, as everyone was taking social distancing seriously. The journey itself was enjoyable, and Deidre always had a warm glow when she visited her little home-from-home – her Garden of Eden, but without the temptation. We also had something good to talk about. Her biologicals treatment passed without incident, and we were both thankful they were not as traumatic as the chemo version.

During the rest of the month we were blessed with excellent weather, which lifted our spirits as only sunlight can. Despite Deidre's aches, she was able to enjoy walks and sitting in the garden. Conan and Suzanne made another welcome visit, bringing food and titbits in acknowledgement of our 'vulnerable' status. We were branching out little by little, and it was time for me to play golf again.

I had only taken up golf in my early forties and, therefore, had no aspirations to competence. Having said that, because of the handicapping system, even players like myself can be competitive, and I have had a number of successes to my credit.

"Enough to keep you coming back," as golfers say. And I kept coming back until 2017 when my father took ill. He had suffered a series of falls, some of which he did not tell us about, and despite a successful operation to correct bleeding in his brain in 2016, he began to regress. Like most of his generation, my dad was a proud man who perceived medical conditions and illness as a sign of weakness, and of being in some way unworthy of concern. With hindsight, by the time we became aware that something was terribly wrong again, it was too late. My mum was confused and frightened by the situation, so my brother did much of the heavy lifting. For me, I dropped everything else except work and was with him as often as I could. This meant no golf, but it was no sacrifice.

After his passing, I spent more time with my mother, especially at weekends, and in the subsequent two years the standing joke was that in one year my two rounds cost me £350 each and the next, my one round came in at a remarkable £700 (the membership fee). I could not afford that wasted outlay and bowed out. Once I had made noises about playing again, the club I had joined a few years earlier, in acknowledgement of my position, offered me a much cheaper, flexible method of paying fees. It was an offer I could not refuse, and now I had time to play during the week. The new normality did have its benefits as golfers of all shapes and sizes returned to the fairways, and I to the rough.

All of this was irrelevant compared to the news that Deidre's chemo treatments had been successful, and she would be treated with biological drugs only for the foreseeable future. This was like a lottery win, and as we were taking in how incredible it was, we were able to reflect also that her fingernails showed no further deterioration and the metallic taste had all but gone, and compared to these, the other side effects could be lived with. All wonderful, and just to be greedy, we hoped there would be no new side effects on their way to ravage her body.

Here we were, nearly into July and what, coming from my school years, I consider to be the real summer. If only the weather would act accordingly.

By this time something else was happening. In the early days after the diagnosis, each period of twenty-four hours had been distinctive in some way from the preceding ones, made vivid by contact with doctors and nurses, activities no matter how menial, conversations, walks, meals and books, radio and television programmes. Everything had a significance all of its own. The combination of our specific circumstances and the lockdown seemed to make everything we did an event in itself. We were not alone.

Throughout social media, jokes were appearing about people dressing up to put the bin out or sit in their rooms watching 'box sets'. We were all becoming our very own 'goggle-box' participants. But now, everything was losing focus. It became more difficult to recall days, events, what people had said and what we had said to each other. I was even, unforgivably, losing track of the schedule for Deidre's treatments or the details of the updates on her condition she so kindly provided me with.

We talked about it and acknowledged that we were both affected by tiredness, lethargy and lack of clarity in our recollection of events or details. For Deidre, the causes were obvious, at least that's what we thought, but as we both had difficulty in sleeping despite our constant fatigue, we wondered if something else was in play. Enquiries with friends and through the Internet confirmed that we were not alone. People everywhere were being affected similarly, or in some cases, much worse. The term 'brain fog' came into the vocabulary, and I was a full member. The rapid onset of the Covid pandemic and the consequent lockdown had left many unprepared and unable to deal adequately with the new situation. Imagine being left in a fifteenth-floor flat with two young children, unable to go out, to leave them with their grandparents and get some essential 'me time'. I readily concede that we only had to imagine it, not live through it.

But much as we identified this lethargic haze, we could not afford to waste time in it. Life was precious, and as far as we knew, life was on the clock. We had to avoid living from treatment to treatment, because the days in between were our everyday lives. And that is all we have. We needed to keep resetting the dial to positive, re-evaluating our reactions to perceived setbacks and remember to do everything we could to manage Deidre's condition and live a full life. It was not simple, but it was worth it. There was nothing else, and you know it makes sense.

As I was growing up, one of the messages I received was that to be interested in one's appearance – that is, *overly* interested in one's appearance – was a bad thing. I am not entirely sure where this evaluation came from, although I suspect some of our biblical education, denouncing everything as vanity, may have contributed. I must confess that through my life I have probably had an often-unhealthy obsession with my looks and appearance. I was too young for mods, rockers and hippies, but in the early 1970s, I got on the counter-fashion train, starting with Bowie, punk, new romantic, gym bunny, and all the bits in between.

In my teens I suffered terribly from acne, mostly on my face, as boils took most of the available space on my legs. My grandmother told me it was because of rich blood, as if this was a good thing, but for me, all it meant was that for most of this time my face was a mess of spots, either coming up, in all their green glory, or the red aftermath of those now dead but still determined to leave an impression. They seemed to know when it was the weekend or that I was interested in a girl, and would come out with added zeal. It became so bad that I was given an appointment with a skin specialist at the local hospital. I arrived for my appointment, telling no one what I was doing, and fully expecting to be told in a scolding tone that there were worse things and I should not be wasting their time when there were burns and car accidents to deal with.

I had already devised my apology when I entered the room and was introduced to the doctor, a quite glamorous lady about my mum's age and with a very warm smile. For some reason I blurted everything out about how I felt ugly, dirty and undesirable, but I thought I would be a good-looking guy if my skin would clear up. As I recall, I nearly began to cry, and I will never forget how she responded, "That must be very difficult for you, especially as you are a good-looking man." *What? This was 1974. People didn't say things like that, and now, not only was I good looking, but I was a man.*

I told her I was too nervous to ask BB out (that will remain a secret), and rather than placate me with "It's your personality she will be interested in" – because, for heaven's sake, I was 15; I didn't have a personality at that stage – she said, "Well, let's see what we can do about it."

Yes, yes, yes.

I took my prescription to a chemist – not the one we always used, as I was afraid of my secret being discovered – and of course the tablets worked. My spots disappeared and my confidence grew. We had never heard of self-esteem in those days, but if I had, mine had improved. I felt good, and I felt I looked good. At last. I was David Bowie, Bryan Ferry, Les McKeown of the Bay City Rollers (more likely) rolled into one. And then the tablets ran out, and the spots returned. What the Lord taketh away, the Lord giveth back, big time.

However, this was not the disaster for my fragile ego I had anticipated; in fact, it was less upsetting, irrelevant almost. I had learnt some things from the good lady doctor. She actually listened to me, she empathised and I was not negatively judged by her. She also helped me to realise that I was more than what was on my face and that decent people would look deeper than skin texture. As I grew older, my skin lost most of the acne scars but was then subjected to the ageing process, but I never lost my interest in fashion and grooming, nor, I concede, my vanity. But if I am condemned to hell for it, at least I plan to look good as I descend.

The stakes were much higher for my partner. She had always been a looker and took good care of herself. Without saying it to each other, we were fearing that her appearance would suffer the ravages of cancer. We probably have a picture of the typical cancer sufferer in our heads: too thin, pale, head scarf to cover loss of hair, and an overall air of weakness. This, as much as the illness itself, would destroy her. But after her hair returned, despite her nails weakening, nothing else happened. She looked super.

The new hairstyle accentuated her eyes and the shape of her face, and the absence of work pressures, ironically, freshened up her complexion. For that reason, people who knew she had cancer ceased asking her how she was doing and, quite conceivably, assumed she had been cured. How could she look like that and not be cured? Anyone who did not know what was happening understandably presumed that nothing *was* happening and that Deidre had simply made a style choice with regard to her hair to reflect her maturity. Maturity. What a lovely word.

These reactions gave her a tremendous boost, and the good feeling passed through every fibre of her body. Being told how well she was looking helped her to feel better, which, in turn, lifted her morale and strengthened her resilience. It was uplifting to watch her regain an interest in her appearance, and it was a reflection of her relief that the cancer was not more devastating. I did not care what she looked like – we had moved beyond that – but I was thrilled for her and privately shed a tear or two.

Being off work and lockdown meant that a new wardrobe was required, and Deidre quickly became a dab hand at online shopping and more importantly, the 'returns' process. I had several items in my possession, either unsuitable or not what I wanted but which I had retained, due to being unable or unwilling to return them. But Deidre was a slick operator, mastering the returns mechanism to the extent that our house resembled Argos on a Saturday afternoon. Trainers, gym gear and loose dresses became the objects of desire in place of high heels, suits and formal gowns. A transition was taking place and it was serving its purpose. All this to take the dog to the park. But who cares? If you've got it, flaunt it.

And the weather wasn't too bad either. So, let me tell you, regardless of our looks, appearance really does matter and, along with cleanliness, might well sit next to Godliness.

We had experienced a really good run, and it was inevitable that things could not stay that way. The terrible turn in the weather reflected the downturn in our form. Deidre was suffering leg pains, and as we were unable to go out, we could do nothing but focus on her discomfort. At least as Conan was paying a visit to his mum, and Aidan stayed in regular touch by phone, each of them bringing their own perspective and magic dust to the situation, I knew I had the best allies I could ask for. They were a very tight unit, and I have always had total respect for a man who has total respect for his mother.

We had agreed to go to the cottage at the end of the week, and, thankfully, with a slight easing both in the weather and the pain in her legs, she was able to do so. Every visit feels like a victory, as the place means so much to her. There is always something to be doing to the cottage itself or its garden, and her family, who only live across the road, are so supportive and bring her such comfort. I love being there too, with a whole new routine and the heavy air facilitating deep, refreshing sleep.

On this occasion we also had the welcome surprise of a visit from our two friends, Sean and Clare, who had a rare day off from their own family duties and had been out for a drive in the vicinity. They are two of the world's loveliest people and they give Deidre such a lift. We were fortunate to have a beautiful day for their visit, and we took the opportunity to eat outside – as a form of social distancing was still required – and visit some of the nearby landmarks. Friendship is an amazing thing, and people sometimes do not realise the joy and comfort they can bring by simply turning up. It was a day we needed.

As the lockdown regulations eased a little, we decided to visit a hotel about fifty or so miles away. Not too close but not too far, in other words. One of the issues we now had to address was what to do with the dog. Although the hotel was dog friendly, we agreed – that is, Deidre decided and I agreed – that as she was still only a pup – Lily, that is – it would not be fair on her to leave her in the hotel room for periods of time. I was relieved to have the opportunity to help get my breathing back to something like normal. And besides, we needed some time on our own.

The hotel was doing everything in its power to make everyone's stay enjoyable, but they could do nothing about the atmosphere, which was different but difficult to describe. Everyone's movements looked so deliberate, almost slow motion, and our masks were on and off more often than Burton and Taylor's relationship. The mask wearing and social distancing within the building was carried out with military precision. It was all well intended but how effective it was, we dared not think. But at least we were out.

If you have ever been to a near-empty concert hall, sports event or pub, you will know that there is no atmosphere, and social distancing in the bar area made this a similar experience. In fact, towards the end of the evening, people looked like they were suffering from a good idea gone wrong. It was not the hotel's fault; they were doing what they could, and anything we did on our own, like walking in the estate, was enjoyable, but when vibrancy was required, they were beaten. By now, I was missing Lily and counting the hours until I could see her again. My breathing had improved, but my longing was unbearable. All in all, not the big escape we had anticipated, but there is always tomorrow.

On Sunday we took the 'Stairway to Heaven' in Fermanagh– well, some of it. It is a steep ascent in anyone's estimation, and I was the more relieved we agreed not to attempt to go the whole way, as I found it tough. It did occur to me, however, that if this is as close as I get to heaven, I am in big trouble. We had to drive through several fields to get parked, and I could not relax for picturing coming back to find that the car had sunk to a depth where it could not be towed out. Luckily, this did not happen, and after a drink on the way back, we had an early tea and retired to our room. The trip did serve to take Deidre's mind off, for a couple of days at least, the second set of scan results she was to receive later in the week.

We got through the next three days doing this and that, and on the Thursday after receiving her biological treatments, she would speak with the oncologist. I rose at the new normal time, made coffee and took the dog for a walk, a longer walk than usual for the morning. I was scenario-building. There was no reason to suspect that anything could go wrong with the scan results, but I was still apprehensive. The first set of results were beyond our wildest dreams, but they could have created unrealistic expectations, with anything less perceived as disappointing. The last thing we needed was disappointment. No matter how confident we should be, there was always a worst-case scenario. As if life wasn't difficult enough. To be confident was not to be complacent, but for many they were one and the same. I was simply hoping. A good result would mean everything.

The stakes were high. If we could get a positive outcome, it would help to build a momentum of sorts, raising Deidre's expectations about what she could reasonably plan for in life. At least that was the theory. Because of the ongoing virus restrictions, I was unable to attend, so I spent my time at home like a sports coach on the touchline – willing the team on, expending emotional energy but utterly ineffectual in influencing the result.

Finally, she returned, and this time I could not affect any pretence of holding back.

"Well?"

"Well what?" Not what I needed at all. I could guess nothing from her expression.

"For heaven's sake, is it all okay?" Thankfully, I received a beaming smile and all tensions were forgotten.

"I had my biologicals and got my scan results and they were excellent. Further regression: no sign in breast, down to 2mm in lung and 'dramatic reduction', to quote my oncologist, from 4cm to 1.5cm in liver. And they are expecting further regression with bios." She remembered every word of that. Involuntarily, I took two steps backwards, as if pressed by an unseen hand. My legs had become weak and my head had fried. I was too ecstatic to respond.

"Are you okay? Are you not pleased?" She looked confused.

"Pleased? I'm ecstatic. Believe me. It's just so fantastic, it's hard to take in." She knew what I meant. I retraced my two steps and put my arms around her, taking her in a bear hug.

"I am delighted darling, and I am just taking it all in. We are so, so lucky, and I am so grateful for us and delighted for you. You deserve it."

I didn't know what else to say, as I think I was in shock. I am not sure whether I had lost the ability to expect things to go well, but here it was, the only thing that really mattered had gone as we had hoped when needed most. Yet again I thought about that first afternoon but chose not to mention it for fear of affecting the mood. Unlike last week's hotel, we had atmosphere.

*

While Deidre had expressed a reluctance to become active in any of the cancer support groups, she gained great comfort from reading and sharing texts with women who were also suffering. The personalities, like most of the books available, reflected the range of approaches, from gung-ho to morbidity – all understandable.

Consistent with Deidre's personality, she steered a middle line and engaged only to a moderate level. While, selfishly, I was concerned that hearing a series of sad stories might wear her down, my concerns were unfounded, as for every truly heartbreaking account, there were, I am told, many stories of bravery, hope and success.

One woman in particular, who had bowel rather than breast cancer, expressed herself eloquently and described her situation movingly. Deidre followed her with great enthusiasm, watching the videos and reading her 'posts'. How people can be so vibrant in such circumstances is a wonder, and can be a motivation to us all. Deidre kept me updated on her comings and goings, and as her story progressed, it became clear that there was not to be a happy ending. When Deidre handed me her phone with what proved to be the woman's final text, I felt ill. I was upset for the woman I did not know and had never met. Of course I was. But I could only focus on how my partner might react when she compared this woman's experience to her own. This is what we do, and we cannot help it. When people my age pass away, I feel more comfortable if I hear they have consumed eighty cigarettes, a litre of booze and three Ulster fries a day, as there is an obvious reason why they have gone. Equally, if someone is suffering from a similar affliction and it does not go well, it is difficult to shake off the notion that the same fate awaits us. To my delight, Deidre gave no signs of being negatively affected by the woman's passing and even spoke about how uplifting her story was. Thank you, woman I do not know. You are another angel, but sadly now one with wings.

Sunday mornings have always provided an opportunity for some reflection, be they world events or personal circumstances. As a shuddering reminder that there is a world outside, not that far from home, we have been transfixed by the search for a missing schoolboy with the tragic, almost inevitable, conclusion in the discovery of a body matching his description. When we consider the pain his mother will be suffering, now and forever, how can any of our own concerns be valid? How can we as individuals feel entitled to good luck or a happy ending when these things happen? I hope that, in time, the pain will ease and his mother will be able to make some sense of her life.

On the personal front, I decided to return to work on a partially retired basis. I say that because it seemed to take on a momentum of its own over the past week, and I had completed the first batch of forms. In my job there were always forms. I was unsure as to whether it was the right or wrong decision, but I think that at times there is neither a right nor wrong decision, simply the decision we make. Deidre, my boss and her boss were happy, so it must have been a good idea. It was not an attempt to return to my previous life. That was gone forever, but I was not afraid of adding a dimension to the new journey that had already begun.

Initially, when I called my boss, Pauline, it was simple. I was going to inform her of my plan to retire. It was a given. However, as we spoke, I was not able to get the word 'retire' out of my mouth. She wouldn't let me. As our conversation progressed, we seemed to construct a scenario where I would return on a partially retired basis, something I had not considered, but something that, all of a sudden, seemed quite attractive. I was particularly taken by her enthusiasm and assurance that she could get it arranged. We all like to be wanted. She put Deidre's situation and wishes foremost, and we agreed that I would consult and report back.

Deidre's response when I raised the idea was the clincher. She looked at me, smiled, and said, "Well, we have certainly moved on from when I wouldn't let you out of my sight. I was even following you to the loo," she laughed, "but I think you should give it a try. I mean, what's the worst can happen? When do you need to decide?" I confirmed that I would call Pauline back as soon as we had decided, and Deidre responded, "Why don't you?"

"Now?" I enquired.

"Why not?" as if it was patently obvious.

"Okay, then, I will." And that was that. We agreed that I could return, give it a try and if things were not going well, retire properly.

This week saw Deidre take her second 'biological only' treatment, and I hoped the side effects would diminish as a consequence to the extent that they would be easier to manage. I hated watching her in pain or discomfort, and that would never change.

11

The talk was all about the easing of lockdown restrictions and when people would be able to go back into pubs and restaurants, and take holidays abroad. We, however, had to remain cautious, as this was not over, not by a long way.

Our lives had already been changed by cancer, but Covid was a catastrophe for thousands of people who had died or lost loves ones and had been unable to mourn their loss appropriately. It had been a disaster for the economies of most countries and who knows how long it would take to recover jobs, savings and livelihoods, when, as always, those at the lower end of the food chain suffered most. There were many people throughout the world dealing with serious or terminal illnesses for whom the virus had brought additional agonies: missed appointments, delayed treatments, postponed surgeries, with all the stress these disappointments would bring for the patients and their families.

On the other hand, experts argued that, as a species, we

had been given an opportunity to reassess what was really important to us, individually and as a society, to live with what we needed rather than what we wanted, in pursuit of happiness. As we sat watching yet another television bulletin, I think we were both quietly counting our blessings, as we had already completed our reassessment.

The summer weather was everything we hoped it would be: bright, warm and dry. The country, indeed the world, needed something to lift it. The realities of the lockdown had taken hold of everyone, at least those existing in the real world of bills and responsibilities. For some – those well enough off to be immune to normal life – I imagine it was simply an inconvenience. For many, the restrictions on travel and the consequent inability to meet loved ones and those who depended on family members or professional carers were much more than that.

Most people most of the time could see the need for restrictions of some kind, and largely, it appeared, obeyed the rules. Sporting, musical and theatrical events had been cancelled, offices were empty, only shops which provided necessary commodities continued to open, and outside activities such as jogging or walks in the park were limited to once per day.

Those of us fortunate to have a garden or some private space enjoyed the sunshine while empathising which those who did not. For parents who were effectively trapped in dwellings with no outlet for the kids' energies, it must have been a nightmare, and we could only guess as to the effects, immediate and long term, on their mental health.

We took a walk when we could, enjoyed the garden as often as possible and were able to rely on friends of the boys, some of whom I barely knew, to leave items such as milk, bread and newspapers at our door. Yes, we still read newspapers. As we could not make contact, even verbal, with our messengers, we kept watching the front door until, as if by magic, a shopping bag attached itself to the door handle with the goodies inside. One particular friend of Aidan arrived every Sunday, often leaving items which demonstrated consideration for us, such as chocolate and treats for the dog. Tom, we salute you!

We became avid online shoppers, and negotiating the Tesco delivery booking system became a skilled battle of wits requiring attention to detail and perfect timing, like playing chess against a virtual opponent. We ordered almost everything from a variety of providers, including clothes – as the new lockdown wardrobe took shape – complete-meals ingredients which required preparation, and wine. Oh yes, wine.

On principle, I preferred going into the shops to support the local economy, but now there was no debate to be had, no moral dilemma. View, click, pay, wait and wear. Or return. Simple. And many of us must have looked great wandering around our homes or down to the park. It appeared that the world was attempting to deal with the situation by immersing itself in trivialities: quizzes, online shopping, television, and whatever sport continued to take place.

For others, including ourselves, there was more to it. There might yet be the anticipated toilet roll shortage, but we feared a shortage of essential medicines. Pharmaceutical companies were pouring their resources into the race to find a vaccine, and it was conceivable that they would have to cease production of other drugs. Unfortunately, the world's cancer cells did not get the memo about the virus and continued working. Deidre, like the others, was totally dependent upon the treatments, and it would be catastrophic should they become unavailable. She had only begun her treatment plan when the virus first arrived, but the media was awash with stories of impending shortages in everything, including cancer drugs. Every time we felt things were looking up, something happened to make them look down, and then some.

It was the same the world over, and possibly only an alien invasion could have been more frightening. The news coverage was alarming, as the numbers of those infected and dead rose by the day, and rapidly became simple statistics. The footage of hospitals and buildings set aside to deal with the sick and dying were like those from a Hollywood disaster movie made with an excessively large budget.

The virus was attacking the respiratory system primarily, and given my own problems, the scenes were haunting. I had survived pneumonia three times, but I sensed that if I caught this one, my luck would be out. The thought of an asthma-inhalers shortage was bad enough, but the possibility of no cancer drugs could not be contemplated. There was no Plan B. We tried to talk about it, but what was there to say? We both knew that without the drugs the cancer would not go away by itself.

While the pharmaceutical companies were effectively competing to find a vaccine, driven on by a combination of government pressure and potential rewards, we could only hope they would continue to produce the drugs that were already essential and lifesaving.

Life, however, continued, as did Deidre's side effects, encompassing aches, itching, and cramps, and while listing them out seems undignified, this is what happens when people are fighting cancer. It was painful to watch her at times, but the effects of the chemo were beginning to lessen, and for me, apart from words of encouragement or a listening ear, there was nothing I could do except be there. Over thirty weeks into this journey, as another summer drew to a close and the nights were getting darker again, we were heading into the first Covid winter in a world which had become barely recognisable.

Despite my best efforts, I could not help but dwell on what Deidre was going through and what her innermost feelings must be. I might be there every step of the way with her, but was not the same. It could never be. I was frightened that she was feeling immense fear and helplessness alone on her own, afraid to share with anyone. How lonely a place that must be. I accepted that she must panic at times, as would I, but I wondered if it was always there, spoiling everything and making life effectively meaningless. Or did it come and go, allowing her to forget, even momentarily, before another dark cloud appeared on the horizon? She was putting on such a good performance that, without exception, people were complimentary about her appearance, her demeanour and how she was handling her life.

As if this line of thinking was not tormenting enough, I developed a theory that she was expertly putting on a show to protect her loved ones from the truth, and the pain that would come with it. She is brave and classy and it was feasible that she could pull it off. This developed further. No matter how close we have become – and in many ways we are closer than before the diagnosis – no one can ever know what is going on in another's most private moments. And that is good because they are no one else's business. She is entitled to open up about as much or as little as she wants, when she chooses, and I will be there to listen and help where I can. I chose to believe what I was seeing rather than dig deeper, because anything else was too much to contemplate.

*

The breeze brushed off the sail, making that soft flapping noise which felt so reassuring. Both the sky and the sea were blue, the sun was already up and everything was good – so, so good. "A little Buck's Fizz?" I ventured, anticipating the reply.

"What time is it? Is it not a wee bit early, even for you?" Just as I expected.

"Well, it's nearly 10 am," – it was 9.35 – "and as I have been up from eight plotting our course and organising provisions, I thought we were entitled to a treat. You know how I love treats!" and we both laughed.

"Oh, go on then, but not a big one for me." No chance of

that anyway, as I was in the 'greedy' mood. Not since Napa Valley in 2013 had I savoured the delights at this hour of the morning. But we were on holiday and everything was wonderful, not a worry in the world. Deidre had been cured, our wee dog was with us and we had use of the yacht and freedom of the sea for as long as we wished. The champagne tasted delicious, refreshing and mischief-encouraging at the same time, and if you looked closely, you could see the slightest dribble of orange juice in my glass. Oh yes! We sipped, stared out to sea and said nothing, because nothing needed to be said. For a while anyway.

"I told you it would be like this."

"Yes, I know. You did," my partner admitted, graciously.

"But you never believed me."

"I know, but I do now. Everything is just as we hoped it would be. It was worth all the pain and fear."

"Well, you need fear no longer, as everything is okay and we will live forever."

This is what we had hoped for. The result of everything we had worked for, suffered for and longed for, at last. Just then a strange sensation occurred which was completely incongruent with the mood on board the yacht, and it's as if I could hear a voice in my head.

"Co… Co… Col," it whispered. The sound was so distant I could barely hear it. Was it the whisper of the sea? The yacht rocked slightly, causing an impact with my leg.

"Colin, Colin, Colin," and my body reacted to the blow it had just received. My eyes were open and I began to make out the strange object in my line of vision. It was the light on the ceiling of the bedroom.

"Colin, wake up. You must have been dreaming, but you need to get up and walk the dog. Quickly, she will be crying,"

"Oh God, yes, sorry. I must have been dreaming." I crawled out of bed, took my inhaler and a glass of water before brushing my teeth and getting dressed. There, like life itself, was the wee face at the window of the kitchen door. She needed me, and it was nice to be needed. As she attacked her breakfast of chicken and granules, I eased into the utility room. I reached down and lifted a bottle of champagne, one of those we had been saving for a special occasion, although I wondered what could be more special than each successive day we were alive. I held the bottle as if it also required my care and attention, gave it a good stare and whispered to myself, "Someday, I promise, someday soon, we will acquaint ourselves." I did not allow myself to be heartbroken at the realisation that it had been a dream, but it was, if only for a short time, the best day of my life.

Another benefit of Deidre's recently acquired interest in social media was her discovery of a network of fellow sufferers who were not only attempting to gain a greater understanding of their cancer but, more importantly, gain more equal access to similar treatments and drugs throughout the UK.

Although all the women in the group were living with metastatic breast cancer, those in Northern Ireland were not the beneficiaries of special NHS services as were their counterparts in England and Wales. They were also seeking access to specialist nurses with the relevant expertise, and to quality, equitable and person-centred care. While each woman's cancer story was different, unique, a common thread was the belief that despite everything being done for them and for which they were truly grateful, they were not given the prominence afforded to other types of breast cancer, and consequently, with a favourable review of priorities, they could be more effectively served by the medical profession right away, with the added benefit of bringing an improvement in services for those coming behind them. Their position was that a comprehensive audit of how many people are living with the disease would provide official statistics and proper funding, and shape the service appropriately to meet their needs.

I did not know if their voices were being heard, but it was something Deidre felt strongly about, and that was good enough for me.

*

In a year of significances, 24 October will always stand out. On that evening, Connie was born. Deidre's granddaughter had come into the world, and three weeks early. I always joked, there was D time, and there was C time. I was obsessed with being *on* time, and in the D world it was enough to be *just in* time. As mother and baby were well, I could happily safely say, "Good girl, Connie." There have been births before, and there will be after, but because of the happiness the anticipation and arrival brought to Deidre, I will always be grateful. There could be no better description than, 'a bundle of joy', as that was what she was.

An old lady said to me many years ago, "The old die to make way for the young," and at both a micro and macro level, it is probably true. But we were not occupying ourselves with thoughts like that. We were rejoicing, and Deidre was ecstatic. What a most wonderful, uplifting gift to receive, giving purpose and meaning to life, all in one go. The baby was gorgeous; mum was glowing; both grandmothers, each with their own diagnosis, were doting; the grandfathers were proud beyond description; as were the father and uncles.

In its own way, it is unbelievable how the process happens. But often life is unbelievable. The old die to make way for the young. Maybe, but I hope not for some time yet.

*

A second national lockdown was implemented on the 5 November 2020 and was scheduled to last until early in the new year, following which a tiered system of gradual relaxation of the rules would be introduced. Restrictions, more in reaction to public exhaustion than any lessening of the Covid danger, were to be eased over the Christmas period, and that was about as good as it was going to get. This time of the year had always set me thinking.

Despite how fulfilling my relationship had been with Deidre, there has always been something of a niggle, but I couldn't quite put a finger on it. We had been great to each other and for each other, and I know she would agree. It is not related to anything we do or say. It was deeper than that, and perhaps that was why I had been afraid to confront it before.

If I were to map out Deidre's life, it would look like one of the impressive roads she has built, probably a motorway, where the two most important points, the beginning and the final destination were clearly indicated, and with any diversions on the way, such as small towns, easily negotiated or bypassed altogether. She always stayed on course, knew where she was going, and how she would get there. She had known difficulties in her life but handled them in the only way she could, with poise and aplomb. Class. It was endearing and intimidating in equal measure. But as I had already acknowledged, you desire, you love and then, if you're lucky, you admire.

I knew how lucky I was. But it was not that. I could never escape the nagging feeling that I had let my parents down, that I had wasted my early years pursuing flights of fancy rather than buckling down and returning the interest on the investment they had made in me. I had been interested in everything, but not sufficiently interested in anything to get it done. There was, beneath my outer layer, an insecurity which tended, unhelpfully, to surface at certain times, when I least wanted it to. Many people in relationships can nurture the obsession that they are not good enough, and it can be fuelled by the partner, often inadvertently, others, and oneself, selecting any piece of information to feed the beast of insecurity. There was nothing Deidre had ever said or done to me. In fact, I am sure she would be disturbed to know I had ever thought that way. It was all in my head, like so many other nonsensical relics, but it was there.

I had been low in confidence at times when we met, and despite an honours degree and two Master's degrees and a civil service career, not to mention musical, artistic and sporting achievements along the way, subconsciously, I could always find reasons to sabotage myself. But when I looked at us now, I was proud of what I was doing and how I was doing it, of being a rock. I felt worthy and useful, redeemed. My head dropped forward as my chin hit my upper chest, causing my eyes to open. Another late afternoon doze. I rose, went into the kitchen and put the kettle on, grabbing a mug, spoon and the coffee jar as it gathered up heat and began to hiss. It must be something else, something worse than not being good enough. I had come to terms with that. But if so, what was it? The granules and milk merged with the hot water as I stirred and leaned away from the rising steam.

As I carried my mug of coffee out of the kitchen, I caught a glimpse of myself in the side window. Not pretty. I looked older, more serious, heavy eyed. I stared at the reflection for a while, not in admiration but in genuine wonder as to who this person was. I shuffled back to my chair and looked through the window at the flowers, the bushes, the big trees and the dark sky. It was beautiful, and it made me think of Deidre and everything she had been through. I sat down, had a sip, swallowed, set down my mug, ensuring that it was a direct hit on the place mat, and then, for no obvious reason, realised my deepest fear. I was no longer worried about not being good enough. Quite simply, I was frightened of ever having to say goodbye.

12

I was immersed in work issues when my phone rang. 'Sharon' came up on the screen, my sister-in-law. What could she want? The last time she called me directly was ten years ago when my brother had just been diagnosed with bowel cancer. What this time?

"Hello," I said, more as a question than a greeting.

"Hi, Derek asked me to phone you to tell you your mum has had a fall."

All I could say was, "Yes." *It's not* Love Island *so tell me the result*, I thought.

"They have taken her to hospital and the medic thinks it's her femur because of the way she described the pain." *She's alive*, I thought, *well that's something*. "We'll let you know what happens when she gets settled, but she was in good form."

"How was she found? Was she able to call you?"

"No, Gina had called up and your mum was at the bottom of the stairs when Gina let herself into the house and then called an ambulance and she's going to the hospital and they will decide what to do with her." One of the language's longer sentences.

"Okay, thanks, let me know and we can take it from there."

No matter how little we might see of each other at times, my brother and I, we were usually able to pull together when a family emergency was upon us. Usually. I ended the call and left the room to speak to Deidre, who, as always, asked questions to which I had no answers. I was only interested in the fact that she was alive at this stage. Despite that, another thought loomed, the additional help my mum would obviously need, and how would I be able to provide it? Visiting her one or two days a week and doing her shopping was manageable, and we had a routine developed. But what now? I had an ongoing commitment to Deidre, I had returned to work on a part-time basis and I was nearly two hours' journey away from my mum if an emergency arose. We would sort it out, but for now we simply needed to know that she was well.

The systems hospitals use, notwithstanding the virus arrangements, can be both thorough and wasteful in equal measure. My mum was taken to a hospital in north Belfast for initial examination and then went to Antrim, thirty miles further north, for her operation. As the surgery was successfully carried out after only a few days, she was then transferred to a hospital in south Belfast to recover. As we were under lockdown guidelines, we had to make arrangements to see her, and these had to be in conjunction with the families of people who were sharing the ward with my mum.

Needless to say, we only had interest in our particular patient, and all methods of persuasion were employed to gain these precious visiting slots when we made the necessary calls. There was probably a better way, but as I couldn't think of one and they were not in a position to listen, I waded in with the best of them, using empathy for the pressures the staff were under, the distance I had to travel, and even the fact that my mum had not been the same since my dad went, all of which were irrelevant and all of which were unsuccessful. So we took the visiting times we were given. This arrangement nurtured two of Belfast's favourite social pastimes: watching what the others are doing to make sure they do not get something they shouldn't, like more visitors attending or greater access to the bookings system; and clock watching, just in case someone steals an extra minute. I was, of course, above all of this nonsense. At least I thought I was until my wee mummy was the damsel in distress.

The Musgrave hospital is the one locals often forget about, with its out-of-the-way location in the suburbs, where people surely do not fall ill, and vague history of serving as a military facility, or so I hear. Challenge number one was getting through the traffic to arrive on time. Number two was to get parked within the same postcode. The third, assuming you did park in the same hemisphere, was walking to the place, again to be there on time. None of these did anything to assist with challenge number four, getting in. I believed that the virus was a real and present danger, but for anyone who was cynical about its efficacy, and let's be that person for a moment, this was Armageddon. The door remained locked as the time approached, the clock strategically placed above it to add to the sense of drama and foreboding. My brother had made this appointment for me, and I was to return the compliment during my visit. It was simple, each time we visited, one would make an appointment for the other. What could be easier?

And all in the cause of seeing our wee mum. It all went according to plan – that is, until I entered the ward. To say the atmosphere was strained is like saying too much alcohol gets you drunk. With absolutely no assistance from the assistants, I eventually found my mum and the desk at which the appointments were to be made. Eventually, in the sense that with each appointment only an hour long, every second counted.

"Hi," I swooned with what, for me, constituted a winning smile. "I would like to make an appointment for my brother to see my mum, Betty Campbell, in Ward 4." Silence as the folder opened. The gates of heaven will open with less fuss. I couldn't help it, "We are her sons, you see, and we really need to see her."

Silence, and then, "There are other people in this ward too, and their families want to see them, and we can't give all the spaces to just one or two." I hadn't been prepared for that. It was like hearing about the starving children of Africa when you have just tucked into your steak and chips.

"Well, I don't want to take anyone else's space of course, but you see, I came down from Drumahoe, that's just north of the North Pole," – no laughter, not even a faint smile – "and I need to make sure I can get in to see my mum." This statement was, of course, nonsensical, but I thought it conveyed 'caring son devoted to helpless mum' vibes.

"I don't care if you've come from the North Pole itself," – *So she does know where it is* – "I have a book to keep to make sure everyone gets a fair chance." Her voice vibrated like the laughing sound you hear when you have just asked for a discount from a Rolex watch dealer.

"Well, when can my brother get in?" I was now affecting my 'I know the manager' tone.

"Sunday."

"But this is Monday." Was that my voice? Because someone just whimpered.

"I know, but everyone has to have a chance." I have been turned away from many an establishment in my time, so I know when I am losing.

"What about that day? Thursday?" I had encroached upon her space as I leaned over the desk to see for myself.

"That needs to be kept clear."

"For what, if you don't mind me asking? It's just that my brother will ask, as he seemed to have no difficulty getting this appointment for me. I'm not trying to be awkward, but it's just that my mum wonders where we are." I'm losing this one, and I am beginning to picture my brother giving me grief for failing when he was able to facilitate me.

"What's your number and I'll give you a ring if something comes up."

For God's sake, this is not a golf-tee time or a dinner

reservation. It's my mum! I feel the righteous anger rise within me. Will I settle for this? Will I leave my mum and brother floundering until next Sunday? "That's very kind of you, and I am really grateful." My account of the incident to my brother will not include this bit.

My mum was, of course, glad to see me, and I her, but it is at moments like these when I remember how little I have to say once we go through the 'How's everybody?' routine. Luckily, there were a few characters in the ward and they are keeping Annie occupied. Annie? But my mum is Betty. Like all Betty's, she is an Elizabeth, an Annie Elizabeth, and they are simply using her first forename. She recounts how her father turned up at the Registry Office slightly merry and signed Annie when it should have been Ann, and in the wrong order, as it should have been Elizabeth Ann.

To Annie Elizabeth, her stories were like great songs: they lost nothing the more you heard them. Well, at least it gave us something to talk about, or more accurately, me to listen to. I want to tell my mum how much I love her and how much I appreciate how well she brought us up, often sacrificing her own material gain to make sure we had everything. I have, of course, told her this, but in recent years I am not at all sure how much, if any, has registered. And that is the saddest part. Like all mothers I have been aware of, she was controlling in her own way, without much by way of formal education but living on her wits, prepared to lose the small fights, like how much sport we watched on television, in order to win on the bigger issues, thus keeping the family safe and closer to her values. In my teenage years I resented this and tried to rebel, but at that stage I resented everything, so she was not alone in my disapproval priority list.

Now here we were, me looking at this frail little woman and wondering where we were going. In terms of the hospital, nowhere fast. We turned up on our allotted days and went through the same ritual. We seemed to talk more just as we were parting, saying how much we were looking forward to seeing each other later in the week. Like many aspects of life, the anticipation is more exciting than the delivery.

My mum had already been tested for the virus and returned a negative. Testing was in its early days, so we were all a little wary of it, awaiting the result with trepidation, despite the fact that Deidre and I had had several tests in our lives and I was a recipient of the annual flu jab. My brother and I successfully shared the visiting arrangements, toeing the line with belated empathy for the receptionist and her book. Our mum got to see us, and that was all that mattered. We then had to consider what we would do when Mum came home.

I challenge anyone to deny that they have not been concerned about the extra demands it would place on their own lives. I cannot. I had prided myself on being there for her at least one day a week despite holding down a job and looking after an ill partner, even driving from Fanad in Donegal, where the thatched cottage was situated, to Glengormley, outside Belfast, on a Sunday morning to have lunch with her before chasing all the way back to have an evening meal and relax. People seemed to be impressed that I would pick up her shopping on a Saturday before seeing her the following day for lunch. In my heart, I felt that I should have been doing more, although quite what, I am not sure. I could call in with her more often, but her days were already filled with visits from friends who could, in all honesty, relate to her more easily at this stage in her life.

After two relatively uneventful weeks in hospital, she was transferred to a care home nearer where she lived in north Belfast. Great news. Great, that was, until we came to understand the conditions to be placed upon her while she was there. This care home, in keeping with the furore consuming the care home service due to the impossibly high levels of contagion among residents and the consequent mortality rate, was imposing breathtaking – pardon the pun – rules for visits.

The hospital was a holiday camp in comparison. My mum would have to isolate for the first ten days of her stay, and although I did not understand how this could possibly be required, yet again, following her stay in hospital, I swallowed two charm-inducing tablets and made the phone call to the home. I am interested in how people, if they repeat something often enough, sound like they actually believe what they are saying. In any event, after yet another discussion, the nurse realised that as my mum was on the ground floor, we could, of course, go round the outside of the building to her room and look in through the window at her and she could shout out to us. Not exactly afternoon tea in The Merchant Hotel, but again it would have to do.

The first morning of this arrangement, a Saturday, arrived, and I headed off on my way, genuinely looking forward to seeing the lady who brought me into the world. Whoever came up with the phrase "Out of the frying pan into the fire" might have had my situation in mind. The journey itself gave me some thinking time away from the intensity of both sets of domestic circumstances, particularly with no mates available to help me let off some steam. Having enjoyed my own company and the silence that comes with it, I was, however, grateful for presence of satnav, as without it, I would still be circling Rathcoole rather than the needle in the haystack I was trying to locate. For some reason, in my mind's eye, care homes, or old people's homes as they used to be known, were always stately buildings situated in secluded locations well back from the road with nice gates, an attractive sign and a winding driveway. This care home was nothing of the sort. I finally found it, but without satnav confirmation, including full address and postcode, I wouldn't have realised I was there. Needless to say, I was early, but this did not look like the kind of establishment which welcomed visitors with open arms, particularly early ones. So with radio on and phone in hand, I sat for twenty minutes until the appointed time.

As I approached the front door, the building had the look of a primary school from 1960s. I should know because that's when I went to primary school, and I can still remember the smell. Having arrived, the next challenge was to get in, so I rang the bell, which I couldn't hear from outside, and rapped the door, and waited. Then I waited and waited. Several minutes passed and the usual things went through my head: is this the right place or did the hospital make a mistake; have they lost my mum; or worst of all, has my mum died suddenly? Mind racing, I could not rule out anything. By now irritated at having been so early and now late, I did the thing we should all do first: I turned the handle, and as if by magic the door opened. Having achieved that, I walked in. After a progression of about five steps, baby ones, I was suddenly the centre of attention.

"Can I help you?" a voice thundered along the corridor, admittedly from point blank range.

"Yes, thanks. I'm here to see my mother." And then I remembered, "Well, actually, I'm here to look in through the window at her." No response; she didn't get the joke.

"You can't be in here," she added witheringly.

"I'm sorry. I rang the bell, a few times actually, but there was no answer and I didn't want to be late for my appointment." It was a bit grand for what I was actually hoping to do, but I thought it sounded good.

"Who is your mother then?" I was about to make an unfunny remark about the use of the word 'then', but for once I practised restraint.

"Annie Campbell, or Betty, as she is known." The lady smiled and a warmth came over her face. It was as if she remembered I hadn't come to rob the place or cause trouble of any kind. I was simply here to see my mum.

"If you go out around that corner and go to the next corner and then turn left," she was waving her arms as if directing an aeroplane into its slot, "I will go to her room and let her know you are there." Okay, this sounded reasonable. I left the building and only then did I realise how cold it was. We were in November, and there was no sign of global warming. Immediately, I thought of the cold, thought of my mum, looked at the building and felt emotional at how it had all come to this – for Deidre, for my mum, and even for me. And no matter how bad this felt, my mum wasn't even the worst of it. After this I had to go home.

From my view through the window, the room looked small but inhabitable, and anyway, she wouldn't be there for long. As I could barely see her and she could barely hear me, our conversation was not one of our more enlightening, but at least she knew I was there for her, and we were communicating in some small way. It was, however, a long twenty minutes and it *was* cold. As I began the ritual of saying our goodbyes and discussing when we would meet again, I let her know that I would speak to the girl to arrange for my brother to call again, to look in through the window.

The only thing to be clarified was when she would be free from food and medication times during the day. That done and our goodbyes, for now, completed, I headed home, becoming lost in thought as my car appeared to find its own way back through the dark, late winter afternoon. Looking after my mum when she got home would take more time, of that I was sure. I wondered what I was going to do, but as there was no immediate answer, I decided not to push for one but rather to look forward to seeing Deidre again as she continued to thrive beyond our hopes and expectations.

I had gone back to work, albeit on a partially retired basis, but it was still a time and effort commitment, one which, to be honest, I enjoyed, as it was a release from daily reality. My absolute priority, however, was Deidre, and it was only with her encouragement that I did return. But now my mother came into the equation more than ever. My brother was already doing enough – my conscience told me that – and my distance from her home suddenly felt more like an excuse than a reason for not calling in more often. As my journey was reaching its conclusion, I committed to seizing the initiative and talking with Deidre, my brother, and anyone else necessary, to ensure everyone was properly catered for. But for now, I did what in times like these I am best at: I did nothing.

When the cowboys were being attacked by the Indians, as Hollywood movies portrayed it, they would circle the wagons, and this became an analogy for when a person felt under threat from more than one source. I could relate. With my mum, Deidre's health, her mum, her upcoming birthday and work commitments, I felt surrounded. No one was asking for anything, but when you know loved ones need help, they don't need to ask. It is that simple. Clear thinking was required, and thankfully I had a rare attack of clarity.

My priorities were obvious. Number one was Deidre, who needed my attention as often as she needed it. This, I reasoned, would also assist her as she looked after her mum in the hope that she would not put herself under too much stress. I would agree a schedule with my brother to see my mum and do whatever practical things I could do to support her: collect her shopping and prescriptions, for example.

I was clear of thought, and conscience, as the plan would free me from the fear that I was letting down the ones I loved most. They did not need flawed self-analysis but actions, support and love. And now I fancied their chances.

*

I called to the 'home' to collect my mum on an otherwise uneventful Saturday morning. I was early, and sitting in the car park for the fourth time waiting for the minute hand to move five more spaces, and looking at the building, I was relieved to be finally returning her to her real home while thinking about what happened to her in the first place.

It seems that when one partner is no longer there, for whatever reason, the remaining partner, no matter what they do or how they feel, is in some way diminished. They are not moping about crying that woe is them, but something changes, and they can do nothing about it. My mum had begun her journey with a broken femur and came back with a fixed femur but with a confused head. For all my mum's wonderful qualities, attentive listening was not one of them.

"How are you doing, Son?"

"Well, Mum, things aren't great, in fact…"

"That's funny, I saw Gina down the street. She was just saying her husband was a bit grumpy over the last couple of weeks. I don't really know Harry, but he looks out the window sometimes when we used to pick Gina up before going to hospital. Gina's his second wife, you know, but he seems like a really nice fella. She likes him, and that's good enough for me. Funny, your brother was saying he was getting another appointment but it's hard with this 'oul virus thing. Sorry, Son. What did you say?"

"Nothing, Mum. I didn't speak. What about your other friend? How is she?"

"Oh, she's doing okay, love, thanks for asking. Liz is doing all right, but she hadn't been well either and her husband is still bad, with his heart, I think it is."

The conversations continued, but now it was different – *she* was different. A light had gone out, probably a second one, the first being when my dad died. She had maintained a brave face and kept doing things which, to all intents and purposes, gave her a reason to continue living, but we knew it was a charade. Her devotion to television programmes throughout the day, from morning talk-ins and afternoon quizzes to evening soaps, kept her going, and as long as her television came on in the morning, it would be a good day. And we had a year's supply of batteries for the remote control on site. And enough toilet rolls too.

I had always been disparaging about afternoon television, with my pompous and narrow-minded view of what good programmes should be. I quickly revised that position to one of gratitude for how they kept my mum, and many others like her, occupied, alive even. She only had very limited time for people who visited her, as the next programme would be starting soon, but as the number of times we called kept her satisfied, the box in the corner did the rest.

Too often, however, when the room was quiet, she would say something such as "Ah well, sure it could be worse" and stare into the corner of the room, into oblivion. We could never tell if she was genuinely content, despite her assurances, and one of her friends, worryingly, confided that she was very unhappy but did not want to concern us. This, naturally, worried us sick. For nearly all our lives, our folks had been together, as if they were two halves of a whole rather than people in their own right. Garfunkel without Simon, Wise minus Morecambe, Ant without Dec, or quite simply, Mum without Dad.

The days immediately after her return home were difficult as we tried to establish a routine with the carers and attune my mum to the dos and don'ts of the stairlift we had hastily acquired for her. She was steadfast in her conviction that she wanted to be home, and my brother and I felt similarly. As far as possible, we wanted to adhere to Mum's wishes, and we were aware of her resolve, as, immediately after my father's death, she had refused to stay with either of us or allow anyone to stay with her.

As long as she continued to receive a 'care package' at home, we could act in accordance with her wishes. If I hadn't already been glowing in my appreciation of the NHS workers for everything they had been doing, I was overwhelmed by their response to my mum's needs. I had arranged a care package before my dad came home from hospital in 2017, which amounted to an additional rail on the stairs and a seat in the shower, but for my mum, real people were involved.

These women, for they were all female, possessed warmth and understanding beyond what I thought possible. In my growing list of angels, they are well up the pecking order. Punctuality, clarity of purpose and objectives, attention to detail, and empathy were but a few of the qualities I refer to; and I use 'management speak' because it is probably more meaningful for these wonderful, life-affirming people than for the high-flying management types for whom it was created. To be in my mum's home when one of the carers was there was a privilege. To watch the genuine care they demonstrated was humbling, and the advice they offered, on my mum's dietary needs or sleeping patterns, was profound simplicity. To discover that one of the ladies held short prayer meetings with my mum during her visits brought me to tears. Maybe, God, after all, was watching. I hoped so.

Despite the fact that we were speaking to each other from behind masks, this wonderful system served my mum well. She was at home, and she adored the carers even though I am not sure if she could tell one from the other. It was, however, heart-wrenching that she could not be hugged by her family, her granddaughters could not visit her and everything became so distant. Masks, sanitisers and Covid became the new vocabulary. Already the practicalities around Christmas were being discussed, and, as usual, I didn't know what to do. To my shame, I tried to avoid it, but the word gnawing at the back of my mind was 'inconvenience'. I had enough on my plate, and by now, as my mum was becoming more and more difficult to deal with, and as she and I were unable to go out for lunch on Boxing Day, our usual practice since my dad died, that left Christmas Day.

I toyed with the idea of inviting her to the house for Christmas dinner but dismissed it immediately as the practicalities were overwhelming. My mum could travel no distance without needing to go to the loo, and as nowhere would be open on the journey, it would not work. Given my recent conversations with my brother, I knew it would be unfair to suggest that she should go to them. I could not leave her on her own on her husband's birthday, so the only option was for me to call with her for a few hours and bring food.

I spoke with Deidre, feeling guilty that I had become preoccupied by anything other than our own situation, but, as always, she was clear where my priorities should lie. Of course I was going to my mum's, and we would arrange everything else around it. The love she had developed for my parents shone through. It was a weight off my shoulders, and despite a pang of guilt at having considered any of this a potential inconvenience, I was delighted that everyone was delighted.

During my next couple of visits I explained what we would be doing, and in the same breath, she told me not to come down at all, as it would be too much trouble, and asked what time I would be down at. It was the old, "I don't want any surprise party, do you hear, but make sure to invite your Auntie Lorraine." I had grown to love it, and I knew that, someday, I would long to hear her warm words when no longer possible. But everything was now in place for a great Christmas.

To this day, when I am waiting for a bus, none comes forever and then two arrive at once. It was becoming the same with bad things happening... very bad things. As we worried about my mum and how to look after her, Deidre received news that her mother had also fallen, but this was away from her own home, on steps, and she had broken her elbow. She had been taken to hospital, where consideration would be given to if and when an operation should be performed. Deidre's mum does not like hospital, no one does, and if she could help it, her visit would be a fleeting one.

For Deidre it became a race against time to arrange a care package for her mum. This was not easy, as the communications had to be by phone, which never feels quite the same as face to face, and the carers, naturally, were already under great pressure. But she is nothing if not persuasive, and as the hospital indicated that an immediate operation would not be possible, and her mum signalled her intention to move home as soon as possible, somehow Deidre managed to make the necessary arrangements and the carers would be available. There are obviously angels in Kilkeel also.

I do believe that while Deidre was making the arrangements with the carers and the hospital, she forgot about her own condition, such was her determination to make it work. And make it work she did. Her mum got home, the carers arrived as necessary and the long process of rehabilitation began.

13

My phone rang and I flapped about trying to turn the alarm off, which, despite my partial retirement, rang at 6.55am on weekdays. But hold on, it was Sunday, and there should be no alarm. As my eyes blasted open, I saw my brother's name on the screen. At 7.20 on a Sunday morning it could only mean one thing. As I went to speak, I realised how dry my mouth was. The previous night's alcohol, but something else also. Dread.

"Hi, it's me. Listen, the carer called me there and said that when she entered Mum's house she found 'Annie', as she called her, 'in an unresponsive state'. Her words."

Despite being combustible on occasions, my brother could be so wonderfully matter-of-fact when speaking about a crisis. "I'll go over now, but I think you need to get down." The silence after those words said it all.

"Okay, I'll get on my way. Thanks, and keep me posted." Neither of us stated the obvious, that our wee mum had gone. It was too difficult to say, so one thing at a time. Get there and see what is happening. But there are times when you just know. And I just knew my mum was dead. There was no hope within me, but strangely, an acceptance. Although our conversation was brief and quiet, Deidre had heard me and knew something was wrong.

"Your mum?" Her tone conveyed that she understood what had happened.

"Yes, it was Derek, and I need to go now. The carer found her unresponsive in the bathroom and called him a few minutes ago and then he phoned me and he is going to the house now and I am going now too." It was as if I were a police officer in the witness box reciting from a notebook with no inflection or alteration of tone. It was as much as I could muster, as my mind was numb. Deidre touched my arm, told me to go and to keep her informed. I am not sure if she realised how beneficial those little interventions from her were.

"Yes, of course, but I have a bad feeling." And I did.

"I know, but take care on the way." I knew what she meant, and I nodded as I left the room.

The journey was a rollercoaster of thoughts blowing my head apart. The time I made a similar journey a few years earlier, only to be told halfway there that I was too late, that my dad had gone; the journey in which I had to call the hospital about my CT scan; and most of all, driving to the hospital all those months ago to hear of Deidre's diagnosis.

Fear of death, and now death itself, had been hanging over us for a year, and we could not have predicted this. Strangely, I began to feel guilty about Deidre, wondering if I had been ignoring her. Had I taken my eye off the ball because of my increasing preoccupation with my mum? That would have been easier than it might sound. Deidre looked great, outwardly at least, seemed to be in good spirits and was active and engaged. Not what we expect from cancer sufferers. As my mind raced, with various images passing through it, my thoughts shot back to my mum and how dark the 7 November morning was.

The phone ringing in the car ended my torment, and Derek was on the line. He confirmed what we had expected.

"Mum. She's gone, Colin. She's gone." A freezing cold, wet November morning and our mum had gone. Just like that. A few minutes later I was at the house but had to park a few doors away due to the number of cars outside, including a police car which Derek had mentioned. As I approached the front door, it was opened by a young constable who confirmed my name in a sombre but warm tone and moved aside to enable me to enter. Derek, his wife, daughter and her fiancé were in the lounge, and they all stood as I came into the room. I sensed they did not wish to begin the official business until I had arrived, thus giving me my place. I appreciated it.

"Colin is it?" And I nodded in confirmation. "It's obviously about your mum and the unfortunate circumstances." Again I nodded. "The doctor, who was here earlier, confirmed that your mum has passed away. I'm so sorry." The officer had done this before and he was good. I looked at my brother, as if for final confirmation, and his expression told me all I needed to know. The constable continued, "Your mum is still upstairs if you would like to go up and see her."

"I don't want to," said my brother, although the question was not directed at him.

"Why do you ask?" I replied without thinking.

"Well, it's just … your mum fell… there is some blood."

"How much blood?" That was out of me before I had had a chance to compose myself.

"She seems to have cut her head on the shower door when she fell." The constable looked at the floor as he answered.

My niece's fiancé intervened. "I will be happy to go up if you don't feel like it."

I was, at once, grateful and resentful. I appreciated his offer in the most difficult of circumstances, but I also felt that as the senior family member I should take the lead and he was making it easy for me by giving me a way out.

"Thanks, Andrew, I would appreciate that."

The constable's shoulders dropped a little in obvious relief. I was never one for looking into open caskets, and right at this minute, I could not face the idea of seeing my mum in the condition that had been described to me. The second the words had come out of my mouth, I regretted saying them, with the knowledge that they betrayed my weakness. It is another in a long list of things I have to be annoyed at myself for failing to do.

After the policemen left and we were on our own, we had a snack, gathered again by Andrew, from the local convenience store. I have always loved sausage rolls, but not really today. We talked and exchanged a few memories, some funny but all warm, of our wonderful parents who gave us everything in life we would ever need and most of what we wanted. While my dad was intelligent, thoughtful and brooding behind an easy-going outer layer, my mum was always positive, constantly thankful for all God's blessings, and as such, she was a wonderful foil for him. She had never been the same after he had left her, and in her mind at least, she had now gone to be with him again. There were no tears, simply a quiet resignation and acceptance that this was going to happen sometime, and as she had been deteriorating rapidly, now was possibly a blessing. We all said our goodbyes for the time being, and my thoughts and I headed off home.

As a rap to my own knuckles, I made a remark to myself that at least I would not now be inconvenienced on Christmas Day. How petty and selfish we can all be at times. This woman had devoted her life to us, and I had been working out how to minimise the effect of having to rearrange one day. As my car took me up the road, I could not help reflecting on my instantaneous decision not to see my mum one last time. It felt like an act of cowardice, and that is no exaggeration. And I will be doomed to never stop thinking about it. Other than that, no tears, no yelling or beating my chest. Just emptiness. Utter emptiness. Is this what it's like?

I had nothing to say when I returned, and I may have been in shock. No matter how much we are expecting someone to pass away, it is still a surprise when they do, and my shock had rendered me speechless. Deidre was understanding and did not press me to talk, not least as her own mother was recovering from her operation at home, as Deidre had been able to make the necessary domestic arrangements.

I sat with a mug of coffee, eyes open but not seeing anything, thinking that here we were, surrounded by death, doing our best and talking about normality as if it were achievable. They say any death makes us consider our own mortality, but when cancer is involved, it is all the more vivid. I could not help thinking about Deidre, and how each morbid statistic must make her feel. And then I went back to thinking about my mum, laughing at first, at special memories, but then crying at the realisation that I had lost her forever.

We took care of the funeral arrangements and accepted that with Covid restrictions ongoing, it would be a low-key affair. The day came, and the weather mirrored the mood: dark and cold. It was doubly unfortunate for the many people who had to stand outside the little hall at the funeral parlour where the ceremony was held. I couldn't help thinking that it was an inappropriate way for Mum to go. She was a vibrant lady with many friends and acquaintances, and while several of them had already left us, there was still a large number wishing to pay their respects. Whereas my dad's funeral had been a grand but heartfelt celebration of his long life – with choirs, tributes, hymns, a police salute and a packed church – my mum's was verging on the undignified. Everyone did their best, but we simply could not defeat the circumstances. We agreed that as time was of the essence, only Pastor Jack would speak, and he did this with aplomb and deep sincerity. He had led the proceedings at my dad's funeral also and was a close and greatly appreciated friend of the family. When we left the hall, we completed only a short procession before the race across the city to the crematorium. As the traffic was unexpectedly heavy, I began to panic that we would miss our slot for the cremation, something the crematorium staff had warned us about, and while we made it, several of her close friends, through no fault of their own, arrived too late to see her go. Apart from their own personal reflections and farewells, they did not miss much. The short ceremony was held outside in the wind and rain, and when Pastor Jack had completed his second tribute and her coffin disappeared, we were left wet, cold and with nothing. Just like that. I remember blinking and gulping, like a cartoon character who had just had a surprise. That was it. All over in a flash. I do not know what I had been expecting, but it was not this. These few seconds seemed to illustrate the futility of life. Here, gone, and nothing we can do about it.

As I drove home, I could not understand how I was feeling, and understanding had always been important to me. I had barely taken in my mum's passing and already we had cremated her. There had been media coverage of the elite, rich and privileged breaking lockdown rules, and while I could easily have been filled with righteous anger at how my mum had to leave us, I simply was not. It did not seem to matter. She was gone, and complaining about anyone else would not bring her back. Even at my age it was a shock to realise that for the first time in my life I had no father or mother.

*

Deidre reminded me that her next scan was due in a week's time.

"How are you feeling about it? Any better as they have all been brilliant so far?" I asked, hopefully rather than expectantly, but I was taken aback by her response.

"No matter how well the previous scans have gone, there is always the concern that the next one will bring bad news, that in a split second my greatest fears will be realised. So there is no getting away from them, no relaxing," she said, leaving me unable to respond further.

I pictured a tightrope walker crossing a canyon without a safety device, and no matter how well it was going, if the next step was a wrong one, it would all be over. I imagined this, but I did not tell her, as it was yet another example of when comparisons would be counterproductive. "I can only imagine how that must be." Although I couldn't even do that.

"While I am grateful that the scans can take place, I do not look forward to them, as the process is frightening, with the machine, the hushed voices and the fear that they will find something. And the following week, waiting for the results, is hell, pure hell."

I said nothing but rested my chin on the palm of my hand with my elbow on the table as my shoulder sagged. Deidre came over to me, put her hands on each of my shoulders and kissed the top of my head. She was letting me know that she understood we were both in this together.

"Thank you," I whispered.

"For what?" she enquired.

"I think you know. Thank you." And we said nothing else. She stepped back, allowing me to rise, and as always at times like these, I put the kettle on.

14

A sixtieth birthday should be a momentous occasion in anyone's life, and making it to that age is an achievement worth celebrating. I was arranging Deidre's surprise birthday party, and it would have to be good. It would have to be the best, and I was nervous.

The planning had begun in August 2019, when we were blissfully unaware of what was to come. However, 'Operation D60', as we called it, went through several metamorphoses as the circumstances we faced changed frequently: lockdown; partial opening up; partial lockdown; restrictions on the number of people permitted to meet; lockdown. You couldn't make it up. Whatever the cost, remaining sensible, I really wanted to mark the occasion, and for it to be something to remember for all the right reasons. I wouldn't allow it to be interpreted as the 'Last Waltz' and it had to be positive and happy.

Some of the more exotic options were ruled out as soon as they entered my head. A dream holiday abroad was now out of the question because of the tight travel restrictions, and this was before we even considered the potential difficulty for Deidre in acquiring holiday insurance at a reasonable price. I concluded that travel of any kind was not possible, as she was on a strict schedule for her treatments and we did not want anything to interfere with them. Anyway, it would not be the time for her to be away from her family. They had been warm and supportive, so this would be an opportunity for them to celebrate her, and for her to celebrate them.

So that was it. I would arrange the classiest party I could. Bells and whistles. Simple. I had done this before, and my years as a lounge lizard would help me through. But now that I had that part solved, another set of problems arose immediately. There were restrictions in place on the number of people permitted to meet in an enclosed space, and as it was to be in November, an open-air gathering was not viable.

As family members would be coming from the north, west, south, east and middle of Ireland, as well as England, and the travel restrictions for each area could be different, it was a challenge. Inviting friends was not as simple as it sounded. Think of arranging a wedding invitation list knowing that you will certainly offend someone.

Choosing the venue was simple. The Merchant Hotel in Belfast, although expensive, could be the only choice, not least because of its location, which was relatively easy to access from Dublin, Donegal and London. We had been fortunate enough to have stayed on a few occasions, once, famously, when we met one of my greatest musical heroes: Bryan Ferry. But that is for another day. The hotel staff I dealt with were charming and patient in the extreme. When we weighed up the options, taking into account the need for a weekend, the desire for some to stay over, the restricted numbers permitted to attend, and most importantly, although I wouldn't like to admit it, the cost, we found a workable solution. They would provide the small room off the main dining area, ensuring the tables were adequately spaced, and provide a genuinely competitive rate for the hire of the room, the food and for anyone wishing to stay over. Sorted!

Working with Conan, Suzanne and Aidan, we drew up a guest list to take us to the limit of eighteen people and sought out their email addresses. I put together a few words, heartfelt, outlining the reason, as if an explanation were required, and the plan, seeking an early response, positive or negative. Everyone came back quickly, and some close friends suggested their partners should not attend if numbers were tight. Everything was taking shape, and I began to picture the birthday girl's expression when she walked into the room with everyone there to surprise her. I felt a warm glow. With the venue, the food, the gift, and the select group of those present, this would surpass any party I had been to, fittingly. One other surprise I had planned was to create a short video of tributes from friends and work colleagues who would be unable to attend on the night, each segment to be around thirty seconds long. My recording colleague and close friend Stephen, of whom I had seen precious little due to the restrictions, assured me that editing would be no problem at all, describing the latest piece of kit he had acquired which would allow him to blah, blah, blah... zzz. But as long as he knew what to do, I was content.

I had several conversations with the events team at the hotel and honestly believe they were as excited as I, particularly as they were aware of some of the background on Deidre's situation. The service industry in general, and the hospitality sector specifically, is often criticised, but I am a fan. We had been fortunate enough to have stayed at the hotel before, but I do not think this entitled us to anything more. It was simply a very professional approach delivered with a very human touch.

I went over the arrangements on my spreadsheet for the umpteenth time, but that is what I do when it is important and I am nervous. The room, menu, video facility, everyone's anticipated time of arrival, those who would be staying, my speech and plausible story to keep Deidre away from the assembly area, even my choice of suit, shirt and tie, were dealt with. All boxes ticked. "The Department offers its congratulations on the success of your mission, 007," I could hear M say as I sipped my vodka Martini, shaken, of course, not stirred. But as each successive movie and book proclaims, "Bond meets his greatest foe yet!" Well, in terms of organising the party, I was about to meet mine.

The easing of the lockdown restrictions had been greeted with frenzy by the social types and the industries who service them, and inevitably, as people relaxed into something resembling normal life, the instances of Covid rose to the extent where newer, even tighter restrictions were being considered. When I first heard this on the radio, my heart began to sink, as I knew the party would be affected. We had already reduced the numbers to only those essential to its success, and any further withdrawals would make it not worthwhile. We would be hindered by the travel restrictions of three jurisdictions, as well as the doubt as to whether the hotel would be open at all. On a Friday early evening, driving home with Deidre and the dog, the bombshell, albeit expected, went off.

For the period from late November until after Christmas, tighter lockdown measures relating to travel and hospitality would be introduced. This included 29 November, and we were scuppered. For the remainder of the journey, I feigned only moderate interest, as we were not currently socialising and, as far as Deidre was concerned, we had nothing planned. But my mind was racing.

They say blind panic can be the mother of invention. A further exchange of emails confirmed what I already knew: the party was off. Almost no one could travel, and the hotel would be closed. There were so many people who wanted to pass on their best wishes to Deidre on her doubly significant birthday, but they were going to be prevented from doing so. Or were they? If I had listened to Stephen's explanation about how we would make a video, I might have been able to answer the question immediately, but Stephen had for a long time been used to repeating himself then demonstrating what he had been describing in the first place.

"Would it be possible to get a whole series of short videos of Deidre's friends wishing her a happy birthday and put them all together into one feature?" as I held my breath.

"How many?" with an interrogator's tone.

"Oh, I'm not too sure, fifteen or sixteen," I lied. It would be easily more than that at a first count, but I did not want to scare him off.

"Is that all?" This was not the time for jokes.

"Okay, over twenty; maybe a few more. Is it possible?"

"Yes."

"Thank fuck." I responded involuntarily. I am in my sixties, but I never swore in front of my parents, so I hope they are not listening now. "I'll get onto that right away, we don't have long, and we can set up a night to put it together." This was exciting. Our recording aspirations reached beyond music to the visual medium, and what an addition to our body of work this would be.

"What format are you going to use?" he asked in that tone again.

"What *what*? I'm not sure what you mean. What format should I use?"

"Which do you prefer?" This was like a cat with a captured mouse.

"Which do you suggest?" I could be evasive too.

"Text or WhatsApp."

"Oh, I see." I didn't. "Do you have a preference?"

"No, as long as they can be sent from your phone to mine, it won't be a problem." So that's what this conversation had been about. But it was good to know we were back on track. Thank you, Stephen. This was going to be a masterpiece.

After I had sent a short explanatory text to everyone I intended to include, I began to realise how much I actually did know about phone technology and the like. Some of the questions from my would-be respondents were innocent and some were laughable, but your secrets are safe with me. The videos were all excellent and moving, and they genuinely demonstrated the warmth and love her family and friends were sending to her.

Most stuck to the time limit we had requested, and each delivered a unique personal message which, helpfully, made the whole piece feel shorter than its twenty-four-minute duration. Stephen and I had a long, at times, painful discussion about how to edit it. For some reason which escapes me now, I was adamant that we needed to shorten the video considerably and suggested that we simply omit some of the contributions. Stephen, however, was equally determined that we should keep every video as submitted, and that the duration was no problem, being convinced that while it would certainly shorten the video, it would be disrespectful to ignore contributions, as people had responded to my request in the first place. He convinced me that it was fitting that it lasted the length it did, and in fact, he had some ideas which would extend it a little further.

He had asked me to provide some pictures featuring Deidre and family through the years, and with the help of mobile-phone technology, this was not difficult. I was also able to go through the boxes of old photos she helpfully kept in the house. One final touch was to add as background music our version of Nick Cave's 'Into My Arms', which carried the message perfectly. When we had agreed the running order, added the incidentals and watched it through, we both shed a tear. It was everything we hoped it would be. Copies were despatched to Conan to ensure its debut airing would be problem-free, and texts of thanks to everyone who took part were forwarded with pleasure and gratitude.

A new plan for Operation D60 was in place. Conan, Suzanne and baby would come from Belfast, and the icing on the cake would be Aidan's 'surprise' visit from London. Food would be ordered from the local top-ranking restaurant, and there would be booze – lots of booze. If we could not go to the party, the party would come to us. As the news had broken of further restrictions, the hotel had been very cooperative, and our deposit would be held for future, happier times. The days beforehand passed slowly, and I had obviously been convincing in my discussions with Deidre, assuring her that the celebration may involve only the two of us, but despite that, we would have a wonderful time. She believed me – about there being only the two of us, that is. I am sure she felt at least a tinge of disappointment at how she believed her major birthday celebration was going to turn out. I am also sure she was reflecting on how many more annual celebrations she would have. But I was confident that a few days of anticipated disappointment would be more than made up for by the exciting surprise to come.

The boys and I disagreed slightly about the stage management of their arrival, but to keep the peace, I went with their plan. Conan and family would arrive mid-afternoon and would make their way, undetected, into the house. To further compound the surprise, Aidan would continue to hide in another room and would appear when the initial wave of hugs had begun to subside.

The morning was long, and I was asked who I was texting, as my phone was more alive than usual. Final preparations were going according to plan, and the boys, notorious for their lateness, would be here at the agreed time. By now, I did not want to prolong matters and could not wait to end the facade and see her gorgeous face light up as it surely would. The timing was important, as I had to entice Deidre to the bedrooms, not for that reason, but because it allowed the entourage access to the front door for their entry.

I chose one of her favourite subjects – "Which clothes I should give to charity?" – and she took up the offer with vigour, but as I asked her to look at my wardrobes yet again, I was beginning to struggle for things to say. *Where the hell are you guys?* my inner voice began to repeat, but just when Deidre was looking at me as if I had wet myself, she observed something else. "Who's that coming up the driveway?" I could not understand how she could see the driveway from where we were, as I had strategically placed her to avoid such an occurrence, but by accident of sunlight and reflection from the windows, she managed to see enough to raise her suspicions. I needed to give them time to get into the house and for Aidan to take up his deeper position.

"It's probably nobody. Are you expecting anyone? Sure, who would call here on a Saturday afternoon?" I meandered meaninglessly, simply playing for time. As she moved towards the door, I lurched forward to stop her, putting my arms around her from the front as if we were about to slow dance. Her expression was priceless. "Just wait a minute," I said, without reason.

"Why? There's someone at the door. I need to see who it is."

"There's no one, don't worry." More gobbledegook. She then broke from my not-too-firm grasp and headed for the front of the house. I realised she had absolutely no idea what we had planned, and if her earlier expression had been something to behold, this next one was worth everything. The hugs and kisses demonstrated the pure delight we all had at being together, with son, daughter-in-law, granddaughter and dog gathered in one scrum of excitement.

But like a singer with an endless repertoire of hits, there was more to follow. Just as she was coming to terms with her surprise arrivals, Aidan appeared treating his 'star of the show' status as his rightful place. To know him is to love him, and this occasion was no exception. The hugs and smiles continued and the champagne appeared, and the plan was for each surprise to be followed by another surprise, each surpassing the one before it. As the champagne bottles became lighter and noticeably fewer, we produced the watch she had fallen for a few months earlier but never expected to own. Again, whoops and shrieks of joy. After we all had a chance to hold it up to the light, admire it and hear Aidan's in-depth appraisal, it was time to sit down for a while. The *pièce de résistance.*

"Could I ask you all to gather in the snug?" You can make anywhere sound grand by affecting the appropriate accent. After we had refreshed our drinks – my favourite part – and taken our seats, and when a nod and wink exchange with Conan confirmed it was ready to roll, the video magically transferred from his mobile phone onto the large wall-mounted television screen.

I have been to a few film premieres, but this was the most eagerly anticipated by far. As the music took up and we passed through the initial batch of childhood photographs to the first video caption, I glanced at Deidre to find her looking absolutely stunned. Friends, family, work colleagues produced the most touching tributes and best wishes beyond my wildest dreams. Stephen's production was simply excellent. Well timed, well paced and, yes, simply excellent. Thank you, my friend. You will never really know what a contribution you made.

Dinner was also everything we had hoped for, although, to be perfectly honest, we could have been eating cold porridge and no one would have minded. Young people produce so much adrenalin, and they obviously donated some to Deidre and me.

It was thrilling to observe Deidre throwing back her head laughing, joining in with the jokes and stories, and dancing as we relived Nice 2019 and I tried to revisit my very long-lost youth. I did, however, have the good taste not to do the dancing bit. This could never be the war, but tonight a battle against cancer had been won. This was an occasion when it could not define us. She had earned the right to feel like this and to experience the pure joy of what life can bring, even just for one day. 'Big C' was not mentioned once, and there are times when this is how it should be. The evening continued according to plan, and some hours later, when I had the opportunity, I took some time for myself, to reflect and allow my shoulders to drop a little through relief. While we could not get everyone together through circumstances well beyond our control, each person who was not there tonight would understand that the few people who absolutely really mattered were there. I felt suddenly emotional when the thought occurred. *So this is what it is like to feel proud of yourself.* And out of the blue, despite being sixty-two years of age, I missed my mum and dad.

The next few days continued to be sprinkled with the good cheer engendered by the birthday celebrations as we recalled the key events, including Deidre's genuine surprise, and how the plan had, therefore, obviously worked. She played the video several times, all twenty-four minutes of it, and in the days to follow, as it was posted on YouTube, she counted the number of views with growing excitement as the total rose. There remains a little child in every one of us, and occasionally it does the heart good to bring them presents and watch them react.

"I told you you were truly loved," I said, and this time she did not disagree.

*

Deidre was a natural. She had brought up two boys, but it was more than that. When she was attending to Connie, her guard dropped, as did her shoulders, and she said all the right things, displayed all the right expressions, and baby just loved it. However, Deidre was able to do with Connie what she did with all of us, ease us around into doing what she needed us to do without us quite realising what was going on. Now that's a skill.

Conan was shaping up to be an excellent father and was already a fine young man, and as he and his mum looked after baby, it was so easy to see where he came from, always in looks, and now also in deeds. I once read that life's secret is to, among other things, dance like no one is watching and sing like no one is listening. To that they should have added, "Look after your granddaughter." Because seeing is believing.

As her birthday celebrations became memories, Deidre turned her attention to an issue she had not been looking forward to. I think she knew in her heart that the possibility of returning to work was remote, but as there had been many other distractions in her life, she did not have to think about it. Now, as the employees' sick-leave clock became ready to chime, that time had come. Surprisingly, the oncologist with whom she had developed a positive doctor-patient relationship, suggested that if she wanted, she could return in some capacity, albeit probably with reduced hours and curtailed duties. She thought about this, but not for long. For her, it would have to be all or nothing. The role she played and the duties she had performed required total commitment and concentration. And without those, there would be no point.

She related what the oncologist had told her, but I did not have to ask her what her decision was. The silence and her expression told me everything. The first call to her manager, nearly a year ago, had been met with shock and concern. This one was met with resigned acceptance but no less concern. Those of us who have worked in an organisation for many years have probably envisaged a retirement of parties, despite our protests, with the tributes and best wishes of colleagues ringing in our ears as we head off into the sunset, or more likely, the Costa del Sol.

But now there were no gold watches, no cakes with 'Happy Retirement' emblazoned across them, no speeches; in fact, nothing. Covid had caused this, and I could not help feeling that Deidre had been robbed of the opportunity to say goodbye in the most fitting way, and her colleagues to say a proper thank you to a cherished friend and colleague. At least I knew they would remain in contact and meet in the future, and for that I was thankful.

Deidre and I have read several books and features about cancer, almost always written by the sufferer, or a medical professional offering advice and perspectives on coming to terms and dealing with it. They have all been informative and helpful in their own way, with each of us drawing different things from them.

I did, however, discover two themes arising: either the 'Stuff this, I'm living life to the full anyway!' approach, or the more resentful 'Why is this happening to me?' reaction. I can judge neither, as each set of circumstances is unique, and we tend to view the world and our individual place in it from that perspective. Neither of us has descended into resentment, fuming at the unfairness of it all. It is inherently unfair that cancer should strike anyone.

From the early, giddy 'Is this really happening?' shock to a more settled pattern, we have, somehow, managed to maintain a level of composure. Admittedly, many factors have been in our favour, but you can only do the best with what you have available, and of this I think we can be truly proud.

15

Christmas was going to be different. There would be no getting away from that. However, as the immediate family could come on the 25th for dinner, that would do fine anyway. The politicians, sympathetic to the weariness of the public but regardless of the inevitable spike in infections to follow it, pronounced a short period of relaxation to help us get some cheer into our systems. And who were we to turn down an opportunity?

Aidan had made it home for the holiday in good time, a phrase we can rarely attribute to him, but the atmosphere was surprisingly good. The anticipation of Christmas seems to do that to people. Some people. I did not want to think about what it would be like without either of my folks, so I immersed myself in organising anything I could. A night out – yes, a night out – before the big close down. A great idea, and the other two needed no persuasion. Through adherence to the rules and common sense, none of us had caught the dreaded virus, and we would continue to be careful.

The restaurant and taxi were booked, and we were like kids in the toy shop. We had not been spending any money, not that there was that much, so we pushed the boat out with pre-dinner, during-dinner and, of course, after-dinner drinks. We talked about everything except the obvious: how friends were doing, how well Conan, Suzanne and Baby Connie were getting on, and expressing our admiration for the new father as he continued to provide urgent dental care while covered from head to foot in what had come to be known as PPE (personal protective equipment), the new toilet rolls in terms of national demand, but this time genuinely needed. It was a time to be grateful to all the people, particularly those in the service industry, who usually escape our notice, and it was a really good night.

Sitting in the taxi, the three of us in the back seat behind a screen, Deidre's phone rang, and rather than leave it until she got home, only a few minutes away, she took it.

"Right... I see... Are you sure? What do you want us to do? Okay, we can speak later. You see, we have been out and have had a few drinks. Is it that obvious? Okay, Son, speak later."

"I take it that was Conan," the clue being that she had referred to her caller as 'Son', and the other one was beside me.

"Conan has Covid. He tested positive this evening." She looked at us, I suppose waiting for a response. And then, as one, we burst out laughing.

"Conan has Covid. What a dick," proclaimed Aidan, and right then, it did seem like the funniest thing on earth.

"He says we should all go for a test, as we," said Deidre, gesturing at Aidan, "were down visiting the other day. But he says to wait until Sunday, when, if we have it, there should be symptoms."

"Well, there you go. We can worry about it on Sunday," I said, anxious not to lose the buoyant atmosphere. Alcohol most certainly does dim the senses.

At home the partying continued with a couple more drinks, and I even had time to compose lyrics to a song, 'Covid at Christmas', very loosely based on the Greg Lake hit of many years ago. Our collective energy quickly left us and we retired, almost forgetting the news we had received, and until then, had feared hearing.

By next morning the previous night's atmosphere had well and truly gone. Tired and somewhat hungover, Deidre began by acknowledging her regret at having over-indulged and we responded by trying to assure her that letting her hair down, a phrase which we immediately retracted and replaced with a simple reference to enjoying herself, once in a while would do no harm at all and, in fact, meant we were actually living. She gave a half smile and looked at something in the distance. I knew we had gone too far and reprimanded myself for losing control.

Then Conan's news came hurtling back at us like a cyclist on the pavement. We ignored the first game, 'One-upmanship', and went immediately to game two, 'Recriminations'.

"How did he get it?" I asked, more to open the conversation, as I assumed it had been at work.

"He doesn't know, but he is thinking it through," Deidre responded, as she had taken the original call.

"Okay, but why did he need to tell us so late at night?" I enquired.

"It wasn't that late; it was only after 9pm when we were going home," Aidan clarified. I had forgotten that we were no longer night owls.

"Of course," I conceded, "but why did he need to call us?"

"Because we were down at his house on Tuesday. We called in on our way down to Mummy's."

"What?" was all I could muster. "Well that certainly changes the picture, doesn't it?" I was annoyed, but I didn't know who to be annoyed with or what to be annoyed about. We had been paying tribute to Conan risking himself to do his bit for society, and now he was a casualty of war. "So if he was with you on Tuesday and with me since, then that puts me at risk." I looked at each of them as if they owed me money.

"But it's worse than that," Deidre added. *How can anything be worse than that?* "After seeing Conan, we went on down to Mummy's…" She didn't need to say anything else, and her words hung in the air as silence dominated the room.

"So not only could *we* have it, but your mum could have it as well," I said to take stock, wondering how we could possibly have seen anything funny in this potential disaster last night. "Well, we can do nothing before tomorrow, and then we will know where we stand. Don't say anything to your mum until we know, as there's no point in worrying her, hopefully unnecessarily."

"God, no, absolutely not." Deidre confirmed. At least that was agreed.

We began retracing our steps over the last week. Mine was easy, as I had been nowhere, as work consisted of virtual meetings and emails. I then remembered going to the Post Office store for food for ourselves and the dog. But therein lay a point. We are sure we have been nowhere until we think it through, and there is usually always one journey, one chance meeting, and that is when mistakes are made. When people are contaminated. When people die.

As we continued, it was clear that apart from Deidre and Aidan's visit to Conan on the way to her mum's, they had met no one. Apart from, of course, a couple of visits to the local shops, and then the friend of her mum who had called in. After an hour, drained and still somewhat hungover, we agreed there was no need for further review, and as we had booked tests for 4pm on Sunday, we would do nothing more until then. Except worry.

Coffee consumed, dog walked, papers bought and breakfast eaten. And much later, Aidan surfaces. The usual Sunday. But it was not. It could be the defining day in our lives, as the potential consequences, all of them dire, queued up to slap us on our metaphorical faces. Our official position had been shaped to agree that Deidre and Aidan had been with Conan for such a short time that they couldn't possibly have caught it, and if they hadn't, neither then, could Deidre's mum or me. It was helping us to pass the hours until the test, but I knew. I just knew.

Finally, we headed off to the test centre, a converted warehouse and forecourt. At least that was what it looked like in the dark. Bright, sharp floodlights surrounded the place and, added to the torches carried by the staff, it gave off an eerie feel as we progressed slowly down the line. Many people were still receiving tests, but I wondered how many were in our position.

We were directed to a checkpoint whereupon I was instructed to lower my window only enough for the assistant to push in three bags, following which he mouthed instructions through his all-consuming face mask. After five seconds I gave up listening, with the hope that Aidan would understand every word and tell us what to do. It was not pleasant, and I wretched several times between the stick going up my nose or down my throat, much to the amusement of Aidan and Deidre, who mysteriously had rediscovered their senses of humour. But we knew it had to be done properly, as there so much riding on the result.

Bags surrendered, we returned in relative silence, but the second we entered the house we had received emails telling us what we had done and what would happen next. The results would be with us early next morning. I am not sure if there was a collective sense of embarrassment at how we were so casual about it all at first, but the mood was definitely sombre. All we could do, yet again, was wait. And, yet again, worry.

"There's a series I think you two would like, and I can download it if you want to watch," Aidan suggested, understandably trying to engage his mother.

"What's it about?" she asked.

"A rich old man who is going to die and his kids are fighting over his business and fortune," he summarised with enthusiasm.

"How uplifting," I offered, unable to help myself, "and then they all catch Covid." We started laughing again as the tension left the room. And the series was pretty good too.

PING. My eyes opened. *Ping.* This one was not so loud. *Ping.* All within a second of each other, our mobile phones had gone off. I lifted mine to see that it was 6.20am. No one sends texts at that time, but I was about to discover that 'someone' did. As Deidre read hers, I read mine. It was the same message. We had Covid. Deidre headed to Aidan's room, and he confirmed similar. We had Covid.

If my emotions could be drawn as a Venn diagram, they would be in the segment where disbelief and fear are together. I read it again. There was no mistake, as even at this time of the morning I could understand simple sentences. As I joined the other two, I had one simple request which sounded like an order. "Keep the dog the hell out of my way!" They understood, as they did not object to the request or the tone in which it was delivered. These were worrying times for older people and asthmatics. And I was an older chronic asthmatic. We had not been going out apart from family visiting duties and, of course, Friday night, so little change there. But Deidre's treatments and my respiratory system were under direct threat. We had lived like hermits, followed all the rules of engagement, been fortunate with Deidre's treatments, and now? Staying away from everyone would not be too difficult, and there were friends who could look after Deidre's mum, not that she needed it, as she was sturdy, even with her broken elbow.

I had visited the Anne Frank Museum in Amsterdam some years ago, as well as reading her diary, and at the time wondered what it must have been like to live like that and under such threat. We were nowhere near that, but our current situation did help my appreciation of their plight. A dog minder, very well recommended, had been in touch and arrangements were made for a pickup which did not involve any contact. That was great. We would miss the wee dog, but I had to give myself a chance, and anyway, we could not even take her for a walk.

I was worried for both of us, as I expected Aidan, given his age, to make a full recovery. I trusted we would come through, but I could not be sure. There had been too many unhappy endings. Deidre contacted the hospital, and they confirmed that her treatments would cease until she was able to demonstrate a negative test with the kits I had sent for in anticipation of such an occurrence. Her disappointment was understandable, and she was also concerned that her condition might worsen in the absence of the drugs. I reasoned that it could not be possible, as she was only likely to miss one treatment, but, again, I could not know for sure. No one knew.

The three of us acknowledged, however, that because Covid was attacking the respiratory system, I was the one under the greatest threat. Images of the hospitals came into my mind, and as the figures rose – even the UK Prime Minister had suffered badly – a phrase came back to me. "Why not me?" I thought back to the time in 2016 when I had the scare, and despite doing everything reasonably possible to be careful, here we were, with Covid. It made me accept that death is a lot closer than we care to recognise, but we can only do so much. I did not want to lose Deidre, and I did not want to go either, while realising that for thousands throughout the world, they were given no choice. Now, all we could do was wait.

Each of us was monitoring the others as we looked for any sign which might cause concern, but as each day passed, we grew in hope that we were going to get through. Aidan was tired, but no more than a hangover would cause, Deidre looked and felt no different, and I was still breathing. We couldn't even claim to be bored, as we had been doing precious little anyway. But we were thankful. When we confirmed our negative results, ours a day before Aidan's, we breathed a collective sigh of relief, and while doing so, Deidre called the hospital.

*

Christmas. The plans were made, and it would be like no other. The boys and Suzanne, her father, Deidre, me, Lily, the new baby, and of course Cancer and Covid would all be present. The latter two were not welcome, but they turned up anyway. In our earlier conversations, we had anticipated a smaller group, but as Deidre was up for it, so then were the rest of us. We all played our part in the preparations, and everything that needed to go well, did.

The atmosphere, food, quiz all went according to plan, and, naturally, Baby Connie was the star of the show, and with two doting parents and grandfathers, and a doting grandmother and uncle, we forgot everything. Yes, Christmas Day remains special if you give it a chance. Deidre's mum was being looked after by her brother, and my mum and dad were having Christmas dinner together up above. It was a time for nice thoughts. With the spectre of death so close for so long, a new life gave us such a lift. Connie, you will hear many wonderful stories as you grow older.

They all left over the next two days, enabling us to get back to whatever had been occupying us beforehand. Deidre was arranging hospital appointments for her mum, I was working and poor Aidan was bored. On New Year's Eve they went to be with Deidre's mum, as she had a hospital appointment on New Year's Day – *we take what we can get these days* – and I Zoomed and texted some friends, walked the dog in the pouring rain, sent my asthma into a frenzy as I tried to dry her, had too much to drink, and then it was over. It had been a hell of a year, for us and for the world. I hoped 2021 would be better, but the next day wished I hadn't entered it with a hangover.

16

We had begun making plans again. As yet another lockdown was moving into yet another period of easing, it seemed safe to look at the horizon. Not only had we suffered a year of cancer, but we had endured nearly a year of Covid, its heartbreak and its restrictions.

We talk about life being normal, but it can never be normal again, not in the way we experienced before cancer. It is, at best, a new normal, a different normal. Cancer becomes a member of the family. It has a seat at the dinner table. It has voting rights in key decisions, short and long term: holiday destinations and durations; moving house; financial commitments. Any kind of plan raises the question we do not want to answer, "How long have we got?" In the quest to remain positive, we avoid addressing realities we feel unable to face. "Am I going to die, and if I'm going to die, when?" And yet, without realising it, a year had passed. Our initial fears were unfounded, Deidre was still here, so how far into the future could we look?

When it comes to metastatic breast cancer, from

prognosis to treatment, according to the American Cancer Society, the five-year survival rate after diagnosis for people with stage 4 breast cancer is 28%. And, unhelpfully, it clarifies that this percentage is considerably lower than earlier stages. This was the statistic I did not want to see, acknowledge or accept. I didn't mention it to anyone else and did not know if Deidre had seen it – she never referred to it – but as she was scanning the Internet for all references to cancer, she must have. Five years is no time at all. If we take 'three score years and ten' as a benchmark, five years amounts to one fourteenth of a lifetime. Not much, and my heart raced as I tried to take it in. I needed a perspective, and I considered that, at times, it is not so much what you are looking at but from where you are looking at it. When I reasoned that very few people could have Deidre's resilience and previous good health, 28% started to look better. Equally, she was used to being one of the 12%, so this higher figure would be a breeze. She would defy the statistics yet again. That felt better.

A vaccine had been found, or so it seemed. Governments and the big drug companies who made the breakthrough were hailing it as the turning of the corner, and as 'vulnerables', we were in line for an early dose. But not everyone was convinced. Social media was ablaze with scare stories outlining the dangers of the vaccine, none of course substantiated. At this stage nothing could be proven. It was too early for anyone to know anything, but it could not come soon enough for us.

On a daily basis we had witnessed what Covid was doing to people throughout the world, and while experiencing it firsthand, we knew we had dodged a bullet. We did not want to chance being lucky twice, and as we were currently taking medicinal drugs, in my case on a daily basis, there was no reason to resist.

We arrived at the appointed times to receive our jabs, taking care to receive the documentary evidence, as it was to be our new passport to the world outside. The certificates of proof of vaccination allowed those of us who had them to start living again, visiting loved ones and socialising. It was as if the human race was crawling out from a cave, thankfully, and we two, also, were finding our way back to the light.

Deidre could visit her granddaughter and mother on the one round trip, we could meet friends again and major events were finding their way back into the calendar. There would inevitably be a price to pay for all of this, not only financially but in the human cost of lives lost, illnesses untreated, relationships ruined, and we may not know the extent for years to come. But for now, routine? Don't you just love it?

*

One year on, Deidre had become used to the treatment plan and everything that went with it. Every three weeks she attended hospital to have the drugs administered, and we hoped that the practice would continue for years to come.

While the important and difficult decisions about treatments were made for us, and they were there to help to reduce symptoms and make the patient feel better, the side effects continued but were ultimately manageable. At the outset, understandably, she would have accepted any possible side effect in order to receive the treatment, and she had been forewarned about sore muscles, particularly in the legs, and an itch which no amount of scratching can relieve, and fatigue. She had not been short-changed, as at times they all arrived in force. And this on top of hair loss and badly weakened fingernails and toenails.

The hair-loss stage was not the trauma I had feared, and neither was the transition from wigs to her own natural grey hair when it returned. Her fingernails held on and are still with her. As for the others, the soreness could be massaged – we had acquired a roller device specifically for the job – and the tiredness had to be incorporated into a modified, slower lifestyle. But the itching. It was distressing to see Deidre in the bathroom trying and failing to ease the itch with cold water and a damp cloth.

There is nothing refined about fighting cancer, and at times we had to remember that these were the consequences of the treatments which were on our side. Everything about cancer is demeaning. Indeed, in her travels through the Internet and some of the WhatsApp groups set up by fellow sufferers, she confided that some women had to cease their treatments because they could no longer stand the side effects. My understanding and sympathy go to them, and it was a vivid reminder of how lucky we were that, considering everything, Deidre's side effects, while irritating, were being managed and were not preventing her in any way doing those things most important to her.

*

The return from our first football match in London in a while, and we had made it to the airport for the journey to Belfast several hours early, as normal, and taken our customary seats in the Wetherspoon's area. So as not to upset the habit, we also ordered the same meals we always do: all-day brunch for me, and fish with chips and baked beans for Chris, and coffee and diet coke. All good.

After we had eaten and settled for a while, I decided I should buy a present for Deidre, as I had been away and she hadn't. A bad habit to get into, but why not? I began my usual sojourn from the eatery all the way back to the entrance where the Jo Malone shop is situated. It is interesting, passing many of the designer shops, how the idea of travel is linked to fashion to create a fantasy of glamour, excitement and exclusivity. Perfumes and aftershaves – although very few men appear to shave these days – are probably the worst, or best, examples. Impossibly beautiful or handsome models or actors look into the distance, and distanced, as if despite earning millions for these shoots, there is somewhere even more exclusive they would rather be. They probably long to escape from peddling overly expensive smells – half of which are vulgar – in bottles that are impractical for air travel, to do something more worthwhile, like helping charities or watching football.

At Jo Malone they at least come up with a feasible explanation as to how effective each of their products is and, therefore, why they are also so expensive. I imagine most people are like me in that they have no wish to understand the information about the product's ingredients and healing qualities but simply have a price in mind and hope to easily identify a product which fits the bill, without coming across as cheap or ignorant. I now start off the transaction with the 'It's only a small gift, so I am thinking of spending only £X' old faithful which suggests that I usually spend more and am therefore exciting, elite and wealthy – I am none of these. Invariably, even though that illusion exists only in my own head, I spoil it by then buying an aftershave for less than £20 from the bargain bucket. I have no sense of smell anyway, and I cannot even blame Covid.

As I made my way back to Wetherspoon's, with my far too large bag in hand, its bow tied, I began to think about the intended recipient. I am not sure if it was the alcohol from the previous night, but I felt guilty about even considering the possibility of not bringing a gift back, and a wave of emotion hit me from nowhere. For no reason I could identify, I suddenly felt as if I was failing Deidre, and it was not pleasant. When I returned to my seat, I described my purchase and apologetically made some throw-away remark about brownie points and good books and the like, and then, when silence seemed more appropriate, I started talking.

"It's really hard, you know," Chris had the awareness to remain silent, "I'm sitting there watching Deidre change before my eyes and I am wondering whether to buy her a present. Like, for God's sake, what am I thinking? There she is going through cancer and what good am I? I can do nothing about it. I've run out of things to say. I can't be happy all the time, because sometimes I think there is nothing to be happy about. What will I do? What *can* I do? I feel helpless. I am exhausted beyond words." For the first time in many months I started to break down.

Chris intervened, "Hey man, you're okay. You are doing the best thing you can do. You are being there for her. You are there. That's what you need to do, and you are doing it." This was so simple but in its own way, so true. I have been there every step of the way. I have laughed when I wanted to cry, been silent when I wanted to talk, spoken when I wanted to be quiet, and have functioned while unable to sleep. Isn't it wonderful to have a friend who knows what to say? In many ways it was my own advice back to me, and it was welcome.

We had found a pattern. Not normality – that was gone – but a pattern, and it was good. Impossible as it would have seemed from the outset, we were doing okay. We had assimilated the new reality and, restrictions permitting, had developed a new routine. Reasons to live had replaced fears of death, and Deidre performed her roles of daughter and grandmother with devotion and skill. They were, of course, built around her treatments, but she had no difficulty filling her day. And rarely a mention of work.

We were seeing friends again, places were opening, and while Covid had not gone away, it was in retreat, and the health service looked like it was coping, as long as people remained sensible. I believe the human race had been worn down by the thousands of deaths brought into their rooms by the media from across the world and all of the associated tragedies. But there were vaccines, there was resilience, there was determination. And there was hope. However, Spurs had lost another final, so some things never change.

I was enjoying my new role in work, and the diversion it brought was refreshing. It gave me time out to energise and play my part again as Deidre, Lily, the family and I moved forward. Together we had survived the initial onset of cancer, Covid, family bereavement and illness and had been blessed with a beautiful young granddaughter. All things considered, we were doing fine.

"Do you ever get depressed these days?" Not the question I was expecting as we were retiring for the night.

"Yes, occasionally, I do. Yes, sometimes," I reflected. "Why do you ask?" I was genuinely intrigued. I had told Deidre about my demons on a few occasions, only to make a different point about confronting issues, but I hadn't said anything for a while.

"Just wondering, as you never seem to mention it these days... and I thought, therefore, maybe you weren't," she explained.

"I have come to terms with the realisation that from primary school, from my earliest memories, I suffered from a form of depression. This is not me being melodramatic or anything like that, but I refer to it as the 'lowness' which I seemed to get for no reason and lose for no reason either. I have experienced depressed periods in life which, more often than not, could not be attributed to anything at all."

"But you don't have any now?" A question more than a statement.

"Well, I do, but I have coping mechanisms now, so that when I feel it coming, I can head it off at the pass, so to speak. But, as I said, it is not a big deal any more and it's good that you never notice."

"That's good." There was silence but the conversation wasn't over. I took a chance.

"Do you ever get depressed?" As I had stopped breathing, I could feel my heart thump against my ribcage.

"I have been a bit down recently." The answer I both needed and feared in equal measure.

"Okay. Can you attribute it to anything in particular?" Asking a cancer sufferer if they can attribute their concerns to anything is probably like asking a blind person if they see what you mean – well intended but possibly offensive.

"I am not sure, but it's like I don't feel the euphoria of all the good news I have had when I know I should." I had noticed this and was disappointed when she was not bouncing off the walls about her sequence of scan results. "People are really nice, but some seem to think I am better."

"Is it like some people don't understand what you are still going through and think you are cured?"

"Yes, something like that." *I* understood.

"And then they no longer empathise and appreciate your efforts to be normal and do normal things?"

"Yes, they think I am better, the worry is over and they can move on to other concerns."

I appreciated exactly what she was saying and felt for her so strongly. I took a chance.

"Is it possible that you are actually a victim of your own success in that you look so good, you're taking long walks with the dog, dinners out, visiting your mum, and people simply forget that there is anything wrong with you?"

"Probably."

"But isn't that really good? Isn't this what we would have dreamt of? I say 'we' because we are in this together, from that January day. I mean, thank God and the medical profession, but you are nothing like what people expect a traditional cancer sufferer to look like: frail, grey, hunched and probably wearing something on their heads, as they have no hair." A bleak description, but I was trying to make a point.

"I think I have become more sensitive about things, what people say to me."

"Darlin', not that long ago you were traumatised. Highly traumatised."

"Yes, I was."

"Of course you were, and you have not recovered, nor are you anywhere near it. And that's okay. You know it is, don't you?"

"Yes, but I feel bad about it. I do not want to feel this way."

This lady demanded the best of herself regardless of her circumstances, and while this was another of the zillion things I admired about her, I sensed that, at times, she simply did not give herself enough credit for how well she was dealing with everything. But that is easy for me to say, as even though I am going through it at Deidre's side, I am not going through it in the way she is. At this point understanding stops.

This was not the time for a pep talk, but rather for a stocktake. Not to talk but to listen, and to continue to try to understand. Deidre had come a very long way, and perhaps we had begun to take her bravery and progress for granted. It was wrong to do that, because there was nothing about this situation we could take for granted. It was not that she was seeking attention, not at all, but hers was a lonely, worrying journey, like the tightrope walker who, no matter how well the last steps have gone, knows that it takes only one wrong move for everything to be over. Cancer continued to cast a long shadow over us, but now, if we looked up, we could see in the distance, ever so faintly, a ray of light.

Good counsellors create empathy with a client. They walk in their shoes, stand beside them on their hilltop, look at the view as the client sees it. But they do not allow themselves to be dragged into that person's emotional state. They are there not so much to help the client but to help the client help themselves. There remains a professional detachment, and that is what makes the relationship work.

A counsellor's role is to understand the client's perception of their position only up to the point where it assists the client in understanding their dilemma, and, hopefully, what to do about it. It is also why counselling a loved one or one with whom there is too close a bond is not recommended. All healthy relationships have a sufficient level of mutual talking and listening, as communication is their lifeblood, but can we ever truly understand anyone else, let alone someone who is going through cancer? Perhaps only if you have done so yourself, like my brother. I am satisfied that I have been doing my best for Deidre and am proud of how I have managed some aspects of the experience. I cannot, however, say that I understand fully what she is going through. No one can, except her, and that is equally true of everyone going through an experience similar to hers. For those of us trying to offer support, it is not a failing on our part.

We can never know, and we do not need to in order to be of assistance. We can simply bring other things, all of them essential, and that is why I try to say "I understand" as little as possible, however well intended that statement might be. I do not understand; in fact, it is probably closer to the truth to say "I haven't a clue".

17

By now it seemed like we could handle everything that was thrown at us: cancer of course, Covid-19, lockdown, Deidre's mother's fall and recuperation, grandparenthood, her decision to retire and my partial retirement, and also the loss of my mum. In 2019, if the events had been written as a script, we would have dismissed it as unrealistic, but now I am reflecting on that very story which will shape us for the rest of our lives, however long they might be.

I think we both feel a certain pride at how we have dealt with the situation. Deidre has been exceptional, taking the blows in her stride and remaining a wonderful partner, mother, grandmother, daughter, sister and friend. She dealt with her retirement from work better than I could ever have hoped, and she even stated that she is unsure how she ever had the time to do her job! Things I never thought I would hear.

The boys, her family and friends have been truly supportive, and their genuine love and concern for her has shone through and sustained her in her darkest moments. I hope and pray she will live for many years to come, because she has wasted precious little of her time, and because she deserves to. We know that someday the treatments may cease to be as effective, but we trust that will not be for some time, and by then, new, even more effective, drugs will be available. She, and everyone suffering cancer, deserves this.

*

"That dog's not well."

"She looks okay to me." Even though I was not looking.

"Look at her breathing. Look at her wee body."

I looked, of course, but the truth was I did not want to see. We did not need another concern in our lives, and I hoped that if I looked away, the need to be concerned would go away. But it never does. The fact that she had begun to refuse all food and water was telling, even to me.

"I'll take her to the vet in the morning; there's definitely something wrong," said Deidre, clearly worried.

Something wrong. What could this mean? A mild infection, a few tablets and all okay. That would be it. But as I observed the little dog panting and in difficulty, she made me think of someone else with a long history of struggles with breathing problems. But the vets are brilliant these days and she is a young, strong pup. We brought her into the bedroom to rest with us, just to keep an eye on her, and I eventually dropped into sleep wondering if Deidre knew more than she was saying.

Next morning an appointment with the vet was arranged for 11am, and as I had several work meetings, I was relieved not to be there. And in any event, a few tablets and she would be as right as rain. As Deidre had owned dogs on occasions throughout her life, I had accorded her expert status and would defer to her on all matters concerning Lily's health and well-being, except, of course, for the warnings about too many treats being secretly handed out.

I had been managing my allergic reaction to her to the extent where we could share the same room and even settee, for brief periods of time, and as long as I washed my hands after, I could pet her sparingly without those awful kitchen gloves. It was, however, convenient to rationalise that because I could not get that close to her, my compensation was to give her treats, and that it has always been in my nature to spoil the women in my life. No one was convinced, but I did not care, as all I had to do was open the fridge door or tussle the treat packets to gain the undivided attention of Miss Lily.

While Deidre and Lily were at the vet's, the work meetings were a welcome distraction. But eventually I heard the car in the driveway, and when the front door opened, I was anxious. I made straight for the kitchen, seeing them just inside the door. For once Deidre's expression was not hard to read, as it displayed that slight sternness which suggested there is a problem but there could be a solution.

"Well, what's the story?" I wanted to get straight to the point.

"She's quite a sick dog." For all her protestations, I suspected there were times when Deidre actually enjoyed melodrama.

"Okay, what does that mean? I mean we are all sick!" My response missed the target completely. "Please tell me what's wrong." It was only then I realised that it wasn't that Deidre was refusing to speak; it was that she was struggling to do so. I held my breath, or more accurately, my breath held me.

"There is quite a severe lung infection which she has picked up from somewhere and they have given her tablets and have taken an X-ray and I have to take her back in a few days and she is not to have too much exercise and we have to try to get her to eat some chicken and rice and her own food and try to get her to drink water and keep a constant eye on her and you'll need to do that when I'm not here and..."

"Okay, hold on... please." I held my arms up as if in surrender. "Is she going to be okay? Will she recover? As long as she makes a full recovery—I mean she will make a full recovery?" This was a question rather than a statement, and even the shortest of delays in Deidre's response sent shockwaves through me.

"They are not sure, as they need to see the X-ray to assess the extent of the damage, but it will take a long time, if she even makes a full recovery. They will call me as soon as they have done that, and we will know better then." No melodrama now.

A lung infection. You couldn't make it up. Ironic? I believe the dog senses our mood, and when we are arguing, our pastime, her head follows the speaker like the ball at Wimbledon, with a concerned expression. When I looked down at our wee dog now, it was as if she sensed something was bothering us, and she reflected the mood. Hopefully, she was oblivious to the fact that it was her we were worried about. As I studied her face, as if I needed reminding, I realised how much she had contributed to our well-being and how much I loved her. Me of all people. We would do everything necessary to get her better, no problem there, and I made a mental note to ease back on the treats if she was unable to exercise much.

I was shocked by how little exercise she actually wanted to take. Lily and I had established a morning routine whereby I would rise after my second alarm reminder and try to make coffee and get my trainers on before her face appeared at the glass door of the utility room. But as soon as I saw her and opened the door, I was greeted with such excitement that it moved me every time. We went into the garden, where she would peep and then reflect a little more, perhaps walking down to the grass at the local school and playgroup for a poop, after which I could consider the mission accomplished.

It was better to do this before her breakfast, because if she decided she was not interested enough in my forthcoming Zoom meeting to help me get me back in time, I could remind her that she had not yet enjoyed any chicken, and once mentioned, I had her accompanying me back up the road with a spring in her step.

Now she came out, meandered around, peeped, wandered to the side garden and then indicated that she wanted to go back into the house. At times she still wanted to play, and if the doorbell rang, she mustered a few barks, but as soon as these rudimentary tasks were completed, she lay down, seemingly out of breath.

Following her second visit to the vet, we had confirmation that Lily had lungworm, which was potentially very serious, and while it was distressing to watch her in this state, we took the only solace we could by hoping and waiting for her to recover. There is nothing better to take your mind off a crisis than another crisis. While there is obviously no comparison between the importance of Deidre's and the dog's situations, the impact of the latter, just at that time, was very high. Lily had brought so much to us individually and as a unit that we could not even contemplate the thought of losing her or of her being badly damaged. We watched her intently for any sign, no matter how meagre, of an improvement while fearing any appearance of a downturn, and for a few days she seemed to be rallying. Surely, the vet's treatments would work and we would have our wee baby back to her vigorous best and with us.

On the Monday evening, approximately two weeks after she was first diagnosed, she took another downturn, and Deidre decided that she should go to the vet in the morning again.

I agreed, and when the appointment was made for the next day at 3.30pm, I was happy to take her. That morning, she lay at my feet as I held my Zoom meetings, and I was barely being able to maintain focus, more concerned about the little body struggling to breath. The time could not pass quickly enough, and when it did, I was relieved that she could walk the ten yards to the car and jump in unaided. Fortunately, the vet was less than a mile away and we got there quickly, but as the short walk to the entrance was too much for her, I forgot all about my allergies and carried her the rest of the way. My allergy was not making me ill; it was fear.

The receptionist appeared to be expecting us and confirmed that she would summon the vet immediately. As I waited, it occurred to me that again I was ready to put my most loved ones, animal or human, into the hands of the medical profession, but it did not seem to matter just at this moment. The vet, who had dealt with Lily initially, was surprised and concerned to see how her breathing had deteriorated, and mentioned that Lily's heart had been okay when she last saw her. She also confirmed that Lily's temperature was normal. Upon checking her mouth and gums, however, the vet nodded solemnly and stated that she appeared to be very anaemic. I knew this was bad but was not sure how bad.

"You will be able to make her better, won't you?" I stammered. Sometimes I forget how old I am, and now I sounded like a child.

"I'm not sure, but we will try," was the answer I did not want. "We need to get her bloods done, and then I will probably need to speak to the medicines expert in Belfast." She looked at her watch the way bank robbers do in the movies. "It's just after half three now, so I may not get them, but would you be able to take her down to Belfast in the morning if necessary?"

"Of course, any time, just you let me know. Do you have my number? You might only have Deidre's, but if you prefer, you can call her first and she will let me know." If being accommodating was a cure, she would have sprung back to life right then. But it's not. I gave the vet my number just to be sure, petted my little puppy like never before, and the vet lifted her and signalled there was work to be done. I choose not to believe Lily was distressed as she exited through one door in the vet's arms and I through another.

At home, I knew it would be best to busy myself, as I had to rearrange the next day's activities. It was, by now, easy to convince myself that my deputy would present as good a session as I, especially now that my priorities had changed so dramatically. Luckily, I knew that she actually could if called upon, and as I prepared to make my next call, I congratulated myself in being so developmental with my staff. My own boss took a little more persuading than I had anticipated, and I treated that as a compliment, but she then gave her blessing and I was all set.

With my work-related calls made, and as I did not yet feel hungry, I sat down with a mug of tea to try to find something worth watching in an evening where I expected the time to drag. I must have dozed, as it seemed to take me forever to realise my phone was ringing. Deidre was on, probably to tell me the departure time for the morning. The vet obviously felt more comfortable speaking to her as they had met several times, and anyway, as long as we were able to get Lily to Belfast, what did it matter. I engaged the phone but could not hear anything.

After a couple of hellos from me, I was met with the most blood-curdling sound I have possibly ever heard. Deidre was crying – no, wailing – and yet, somehow, trying to speak. In that split second, I hoped she was being over the top, but I knew it could only mean one thing.

Somehow, in all the noise, I managed to hear, loud and clear, the words telling me that Lily had passed away. After that, I heard nothing. And felt nothing. What else was there to hear and feel? While my brain could not interpret this news, the rest of my body was reacting to it. Involuntarily, I shot upright and felt a pain through my legs, stomach and heart that was beyond muscular. We both cried to each other, and then, when we accepted that this was achieving nothing, we hung up, each of us retreating to our own private, solitary grief.

Only now was the full meaning of the news beginning to sink in. After all these years of vacant 'That's terrible, now what's for dinner' reactions to the tragic news of others did empathy with their anguish take effect. It was so painful, so unfair, and what would it do to Deidre? The role the dog had come to play in our lives had kept us going at times, and what would happen now? But for right now, I could not see past my own grief and the realisation that, yet again, I was powerless.

From the tips of my toes through my legs, abdomen, heart, chest and to my vocal cords, I unleashed one long scream of anguish. For the dog, yes, but also for the other painful events which had taken place over the past few years and the unfairness of it all: Deidre's cancer, my mum's fall and subsequent death which we could not mourn properly; even my dad's death four years' ago; Deidre's mum's situation and the toll on both of them; even the restrictions of lockdown which were eating away at the best remaining years of our lives together; all the shock, all the smiling and being reasonable. For what, when a little puppy, brought into our lives to cheer us up, is prematurely taken from us?

One large exorcism of frustration, anger and fear had exploded from me, shaking my frame and my very existence, followed by the sobs of a baby. I had no one to look after tonight, and I could let it go. I fell to my knees and my forehead hit the floor. Sometime after that, I am not sure how long, exhausted, I rested my head on the kitchen table and thought of nothing until I realised I had better take my contact lenses out, that is if they have not already been melted by the ferocity of my tears.

When that was done and I was breathing more steadily, against a background of overwhelming silence, I overcooked some pasta and burned several pieces of chicken and tomato sauce. It would probably have been tastier to eat the packet. I texted a few people whom I knew would understand, telling them the basic facts of the news and asking them not to call as I would be unable to speak. I was right, they did understand and they didn't call.

I thought about the times, shortly after Lily's arrival, when I suffered regular coughing attacks and breathlessness, and I considered how much easier it would be for me if she were no longer at the house. I didn't need to feel guilty, as these feelings lasted for no longer than a nanosecond and we had developed a relationship which was enjoyable and fulfilling. Somehow, I had managed my breathing, and with care and some restraint, we got there. And now it was gone.

As I began to collect my thoughts and consider some distractions, I remembered Deidre and how she might be struggling to cope, also on her own, and I was concerned as to how she might handle her grief once the shock had subsided. She had been through enough already over the past year or so, and it was cruel that this should happen, so suddenly and so painfully. I simply could not understand why it should happen to her; why it should happen to us.

At a time of grief it is easy to feel sorry for oneself. We had lots to be thankful for, but not right now. Deidre would be impossible to console, and I had lost the only pet I had ever owned – not counting Bill and Ben, my goldfish when I was five years old – and was ever likely to have. Yet another female to put a stake through my heart.

Grief tends to take us to the place where we inflict our own wounds, be it the old song, the dog-eared letter or the fading photograph. And we recriminate, "What did we do wrong? How could we have been so stupid?" And then we make promises driven by emotion, "I will never have a pet again. I cannot do it to Deidre," and I was not sure, just then, if I could do it to myself.

Then my phone rang again. Who wanted me to speak to

them now? Did they not understand that I meant it in my texts? I glanced at my phone's screen to ascertain who the rubbernecker was, but it was Deidre. There was no way I could not take this call, no matter how difficult it might be. Needless to say, I was apprehensive, probably because I had no words of comfort to offer her. Indeed, I needed some myself, but I was not anticipating any. I pressed the green button.

"Don't say anything; hear me out." The voice was surprisingly strong.

Oh God, now what? I couldn't help thinking through the thick fog in my brain. The tearfulness was still there, but she was coherent.

"I went to the harbour to be on my own, as I had to get away and cry to myself."

"Yes, of course." I could relate to that.

"When I was there, I noticed a woman get out of her car with two old Shih Tzus and a little pup in a pouch on her chest. I couldn't help noticing the pup."

I sat forward, anticipation and apprehension battling out a draw in my emotions.

"When the woman came back, after twenty-five minutes or so, I thought I should explain to her why I was crying, in case she got the impression I was mad or was going to do something silly. When I spoke to her, she was very understanding and I couldn't help myself."

"I am listening." I could hardly do anything else, but I was intrigued.

"I asked her when she got the pup, and when she said yesterday, I asked if there were any more available. She said no but that her son's Shih Tzu also had a litter and there was a female available…. and I'm going tomorrow at twelve to see it. Sorry I didn't consult you, but it all happened so quickly and I didn't want to miss the chance."

Me? I think I was on the floor looking at the ceiling.

"What do you think?"

Think? I could hardly breathe. "Well, what do you think? I am not against it; definitely not. So you will go to see her tomorrow?"

"You will never believe this either. The lady does not have a mobile, and as neither of us had a pen, she had to take my number on a pillow, written with a big heavy marker. Then, when she sent me the number of the guy, he said he would not be free tomorrow at twelve, so I said that as I live in Derry, this would be my only chance; I would not be able to see the pup." Deidre was at full speed, and I was caught in the slipstream. "Then he called back to say his wife would be able to be at the house tomorrow, so I am able to go after all." I couldn't help feeling that this was all happening very quickly, but maybe that was a good thing. "What do you think I should do?"

"You will know, darling. You will know." Of that, I had absolutely no doubt. In my head, I decided there were places I would try not to go tonight, disloyalty to Lily being one of them.

I thought of a parent being asked to identify their favourite child and settled myself, but only a little, by concluding that we could love both dogs equally and that they were not in competition, nor were they to be compared. I

272

suppose you can tell yourself anything, but it's only what you know to be true that counts. And only you will know.

I must have slept at some stage during the night, but when I rose, all I could think about was twelve o'clock and what would happen then. I received some more texts and emails of condolence, and while I was grateful for people's thoughts and understanding, I was too tired to take it all in, as despite being inconsolable, we were now looking at another pup. I did not call or text, as Deidre would be busy enough with her mum, but by now I admitted to myself that I would be disappointed if she did not like the dog. My intrigue had turned to desire.

At 12.15pm my phone buzzed with incoming photos, and as I opened them, I saw a beautiful woman, so obviously tired, with eyes that until recently had been tear filled, holding a gorgeous, tiny puppy dog, also with a wee sad face. Deidre knew; I just knew she knew.

When I did speak with her, later that day, she was already developing lists of names. Apparently, the owner's family had been calling her Lisa, pronounced Lie-sa, but this was clearly not approved of and a name change was on the agenda, despite the fact that Deidre had forgotten to tell me we were taking her.

Of the names proposed, I could offer none myself, as I did not have the energy, but the one which seemed to stick out for us both was Molly, and at least I could imagine myself shouting it out loud at the local park. Molly would be coming to be with us in her new home in ten days' time, and we would deal with it as we had dealt with everything in this most eventful of years. Lily would be mourned and would never be replaced, but Molly would be welcomed and would take her own unique place in our hearts. That is the way the world works when it is working properly.

When this journey began, I knew there was a story to be told, and it is a story dedicated to heroes: Deidre and all cancer sufferers; those closest to them who do everything they can for their loved ones; friends who have brought so much support when it is most needed; acquaintances, whose acts of kindness, often unrequested, have been more appreciated than they will ever know; people who simply enquire as to how a sufferer is doing, as these do not go unnoticed; the medical profession, whose dedication, competence and honest-to-God humanity should forever be a shining light as we make the slow post-Covid return to normality; even the drug companies, for all their apparent greed and exploitation, have made it possible to extend and improve the quality of the lives of so many sufferers.

There is only one villain in this piece with its evil plan to destroy humanity: cancer, as it steals parents from children, children from parents, loved one from loved one, devastating families throughout history.

This worst of periods has brought out the best in so many people, most of all the remarkable Deidre, who, because of her reserved nature, would never tell her own story, but if it brings any help to others in similar positions, those whose journeys may be different in some ways but who will face similar shock, anguish, fear and uncertainty, it is a story worth telling. You are in our thoughts.

What of the future? Will Deidre and I live happily ever after? Will we get over Lily and love Molly? Will there be more grandchildren? Those stories are for another day, and who knows? But there is one thing I learnt from all of this, one thing I do know.

There is always hope.

Postscript

Over two years have passed since I stopped writing, and I was persuaded to provide an update on the people and events so close to our lives in my account. Well, here it is.

Molly has achieved the unachievable: she has replaced Lily in our hearts and has at least as large a group of admirers as her big sister in puppy heaven. Connie has a little brother Rory, and Deidre is besotted with them both equally. Deidre's mum has recovered fully. Spurs have not yet won a trophy, but as I have said before, there is always hope. I traded in my Porsche for, yes, another Porsche, and we have been blessed to have been able to travel extensively, spend valuable time with friends and family, and do the best we can.

Deidre herself has remained an inspiration to us all and is currently living her life to the full in her third year of remission. She and I have a great time together and we are grateful. Long may that continue.

Sadly, there are a number of friends and acquaintances

Deidre made during her cancer journey who have not been so fortunate, and it is to their memory and their families that the good wishes contained within this account are dedicated.

This book is printed on paper from sustainable sources managed under the Forest Stewardship Council (FSC) scheme.

It has been printed in the UK to reduce transportation miles and their impact upon the environment.

For every new title that Troubador publishes, we plant a tree to offset CO_2, partnering with the More Trees scheme.

For more about how Troubador offsets its environmental impact, see www.troubador.co.uk/sustainability-and-community